HOPE
IN THE
VALLEY

*The Inspirational Account of a
Woman's Miraculous Rescue from Near-Death*

Hope in the Valley

*The Inspirational Account of a
Woman's Miraculous Rescue from Near-Death*

Hilary Taylorson

Copyright © 2022 Hilary Taylorson

All rights reserved.
No part of this publication may be reproduced, distributed or transmitted in any form or by any means, including photocopying, recording, or other electronic or mechanical methods, without the prior written permission of the author and publisher, except in the case of brief quotations embodied in reviews and certain other non-commercial uses permitted by copyright law

Scripture taken from the New King James Version®.
Copyright © 1982 by Thomas Nelson.
Used by permission. All rights reserved

Scripture quotations marked (NLT) are taken from the *Holy Bible*, New Living Translation, copyright ©1996, 2004, 2015 by Tyndale House Foundation. Used by permission of Tyndale House Publishers, Carol Stream, Illinois 60188. All rights reserved

DEDICATION

To my amazing family,

I have decided that this year I will resist taking a three-month holiday at the local hospital so that you could all enjoy the summer!

Turn your mobiles off (no hospitals will be ringing this year) and go grab yourselves an ice-cream.

I love you!

Hope in the Valley

ACKNOWLEDGEMENTS

There will never be enough words to express my gratitude to all who have been part of my journey over this past year. Without God I would not be here today to tell my story of hope in Him.

I want to express my thanks to everyone who has been a part of this book coming to fruition but specifically to:-

All the prayer warriors who took the time to pray for a miracle I am deeply grateful- thank you!

Pastor Karen Ashworth of Bangor Community Church for your love, prayers, support, teaching and your hugs! Thank you for being faithful in what God has called you do. I am privileged to have you in my life.

Sue Sundstrom, writing coach of Accomplished Authors programme and editor. Thank you Sue for your time, expertise and believing in me.

Heather Neill thank you for your friendship, your encouragement, prayers over the years and making it to the end of the book. You are clothed with strength and a mighty warrior.

Carol Savage for your friendship, Godly counsel, love and prayers over the years. You are the epitome of the Proverbs 31 woman. Thank you for taking the time to read the book.

Finally, to all the medical and nursing team at the Ulster Hospital Dundonald Intensive Care Unit, Ward 3A, and to the Community Rehab Team Ards Hospital thank you for your expertise and care.

CONTENTS

Dedication v
Acknowledgements vii
Introduction 1
Chapter 1: God Where Are You? 5
Chapter 2: The White Room 15
Chapter 3: Hope in His Presence 19
Chapter 4: The Lion Roars 29
Chapter 5: Time 39
Chapter 6: The Victory Clap 49
Chapter 7: Hello Lazarus 55
Chapter 8: It's Ok to Cry 65
Chapter 9: God Goals 73
Chapter 10: Pigs and Windmills 83
Chapter 11: Hope in His Goodness 93
Chapter 12: Dare to Hope 103

Hope in the Valley

INTRODUCTION

How I would love to be able to say that I am a stranger to trauma, not every day struggles -but real trauma- unfortunately, I can't.

Since early childhood I have been through a few traumatic life events including the loss of my mum at a young age to cancer, enduring years of physical abuse from my father to being caught up in a bomb explosion at the hospital where I worked. Despite all of this I had remained hopeful up to this present day – but my hope was to be tested like never before.

A new year, a new decade.

It brought such hope to many, myself included. As clocks chimed at midnight and the world entered 2020 with fireworks dazzling in the sky, nobody could imagine how our lives would soon be drastically transformed.

Within the first few months of 2020 the world changed with the emergence of a new virus called Covid-19. First reports from

China in January 2020 spoke of an unknown virus but as the days passed by and infection rates soared, people began to listen. Pictures emerged of hospitals at breaking point trying to cope with the influx of people with staff enduring the most horrific scenes of trying to treat patients in corridors.

Fear gripped the world as the infection raged on and death rates rose. It all seemed surreal until it reached our shores- now the reality of this virus was to enter the lives of millions and unfortunately claim lives, leaving a trail of devastation in families.

The words of a song filled every corner of the room with expectation and hope. It screamed that there was always hope and a reason to praise God even in the midst of difficult circumstances in life.

As the song progressed, the floodgates opened and the hot tears fell rapidly down my cheeks.

How could I praise God right now when my life had been turned upside down?

How could I hope for better days to come?

It was three months since the battle began - a battle of such ferocity - relentless in its objective to destroy my life. It began with just four words -

"Your test is positive."

I wasn't surprised. It was July 2021 and I had been working throughout the pandemic as a nurse in a health centre. This

Introduction

particular day I was covering annual leave and worked alongside a colleague who tested positive to covid-19 on a lateral flow test that same afternoon. Within days of isolating at home the symptoms began and the speed of escalation would impact my life and that of my family beyond anything which we could ever have imagined.

I was determined to overcome every obstacle which stood in my way. 'Refuse to quit' had always been my motto and now more than ever I needed to remind myself of that. I couldn't do this alone - I needed God. I always did but now it wasn't enough to just know that God was good. I needed more than that. I needed to be unwavering in my stance of who God was.

In hindsight, the past decade had been pivotal in laying and cementing those foundations through attending Rhema Bible Training Centre, being a life group leader and occasionally teaching classes for believers in my local church. I knew God was my deliverer, my healer and my strength but I had never been in a situation like this before. I had never faced such a traumatic event resulting in 54 days in an intensive care unit.

If you have been through a trauma or you know somebody who has, then this book is for you.

It is not a self- help or counselling book; however, it is a book which recounts my personal experience of holding onto hope when there was no hope.

It is a hope that is founded on the source of hope itself - God. (Romans 1: v13, New Living Translation)

It is a hope that is anchored in the character of God. A faithful, loving, miracle-working God who shows up in the middle of the storm and brings about change.

When doctors said there was no hope, God was hope and will always be hope.

What God did for me He can do for you.

As you read this book, my prayer is that that you will discover God, the source of hope, and be encouraged that there is hope in the valley.

Chapter 1

GOD WHERE ARE YOU?

The shrill of the telephone shattered the silence in the house. I crept out onto the landing trying to avoid any creaky floorboards. I could hear Dad's hushed tone as I crawled towards the top of the stairs. I couldn't risk being seen but I knew that this call wasn't good - whatever 'it' was.

The receiver was gently placed back and I scurried back into the bedroom just in case Dad came upstairs. Relaying the snippets from the conversation to my siblings, I voiced my concerns about what the phone call was about. My brother shouted at me - but I knew I was right - somehow, I just did.

A few days later my siblings and I were called into the living room by Dad, only to see our nanny and aunt sitting there too.

I looked on the faces of those in the room – my nanny looked paler than usual and her eyes were red. I quickly looked at my aunt. Her eyes were red too. The next part is a blur but I remember being pulled onto someone's knee before Dad spoke in quite a manner of fact voice.

Mum was dead.

Those three words shattered our world in an instant.

My brother was ten and my twin sister and I were eight.

How were we going to grow up without a mum?

I do remember that there were subtle changes in the house over the previous years. I remember a summer when my grandad would arrive at the house early in the morning while mum went out. We loved those sunny, summer days because he walked us down to the newspaper shop and got his daily paper and we were allowed to get a treat of a Mr Frosty ice lolly and a bag of crisps. On returning home Grandad became engrossed in his paper, occasionally dozing in the deck chair, while we played until Mum came home.

There was another occasion when Mum went to stay with Nanny which I can only assume was when she was receiving her cancer treatment. Of that time there are two particular memories which stick in my head.

The first one was falling in the stream beside the flats where Nanny lived. We used to cycle out of our street, downhill on the next street and always attempted to cross the one-way road

God Where Are You?

without stopping, willing the traffic away. This brought us to an opening at the stream. Here the bikes were left and by jumping across that we were at the back of the flats.

On this particular day when I jumped, I missed the bank on the other side and fell into the stream. Bedraggled, I went and knocked on the door of the flat and came face to face with Nanny who promptly put me into the bath before I was sent home by the proper route.

Another incident was when my brother, sister and I were playing in the garden with the bikes. The bike was turned upside down and I was nominated to get blades of grass and hold on top of the back wheel. They then turned the pedals by hand as quick as they could to see how long it would take to break the grass. How we ever thought up of a game like this is baffling, but we did, and it was going so well. That is until they kept getting quicker and quicker until my hand slipped and my finger became embedded between the chain and the sprockets (or as I call it -the spiky things the chain goes on).

No doubt my screams and the blood was what brought a hasty end to the game as I ran inside to Dad. I remember saying that I didn't want to go to hospital but as we clambered into the car, I thought everything would be okay because Dad had said that we were going to see our aunt. What he omitted to say was that my aunt was working that day in the A&E department!

One injection into my leg, stitches and an enormous bandage on my finger later we emerged. My finger was throbbing and I was feeling pretty sorry for myself. I do remember that there was a visit to Mum and Nanny to show them the battle wounds. Needless to say, that stunt we pulled was never attempted again.

Now life as we knew it was about to radically change and there was nothing that could have prepared us for that change. It seemed to happen almost overnight. The only comfort in those initial days and months was knowing that Mum loved the Lord and that she was in heaven. I knew that, even though I wasn't a believer at that age, that I would see her again. That was the hope that I clung to over the next nine years.

Unlike today, there was no support for children who were grieving the loss of a parent through cancer. I'm sure I did cry when I was by myself but it seemed that it was a taboo subject with Dad. I don't recall having any conversations about Mum and her death with him until a few years later when he was trying to get us to go and visit her grave. By then I was adamant that if I went to the grave, it certainly wouldn't be with him. Harsh as that sounds, even in those short few years I wanted to go with somebody who loved me and cared for me - not a man who was abusive physically, emotionally and spiritually.

Every day was a day walking on eggshells trying to gauge Dad's mood as he came in through the back door from work. Was he in a bad mood? Would we bear the brunt of that mood? Was the dinner which we had made satisfactory - or more to the point - was it ready to be plated and handed to him as he arrived home? Could we get through dinner and then scurry up to our rooms for the rest of the night?

Fear was now a constant factor in life, waiting for the next eruption of anger which exploded at any time of day and for any reason. Most episodes included shouting and a physical beating with mostly a leather soled slipper.

Lunchtime for school was a packed lunch in a blue Tupperware box, sandwiches of white bread with a filling of cheese, ham, banana or apple sandwiches. The drink of juice was in a glass Lucozade bottle made up from the night before. Every day we left the box and bottle out to be washed.

One night while I was lying in bed, Dad began angrily shouting at my sister, demanding that we came downstairs. A bottle was missing. The tirade continued as we looked in schoolbags only to discover that my sister had left hers in school. Standing in our nightdresses, my sister bore the brunt of this outburst, resulting in bruising which she had to cover up for school. Meanwhile he smashed the remaining two bottles on the floor at our feet and we were made to clean up the mess. Kneeling on the cold kitchen tiles on our bare knees, we used the dustpan and brush to quickly clean up, then scurried off back to the bedroom. I remember my knees having spots of blood over them where I had kneeled on shards of glass. Thankfully we weren't disturbed again that night and finally got some sleep before school the following day.

This is only one example of what we had to endure.

Another time I remember when there was a fireworks display nearby. Cars had filled the street, belonging to those who were walking the rest of the way. There was a knock at the door. Dad answered and quickly I heard the door close. When he came back in, his eyes were bulging.

He started shouting and asking me if I had made plans for the night. I hadn't. He spat out his words that two boys from school had been at the door looking to see if I wanted to go with them to the display. I just knew another beating was inevitable. I didn't even get time to say anything when I was pulled out of my chair and literally thrown full force against the living room wall (which was brick), and my head bounced off it. The fists pounded into my body as I tried to protect myself. I don't remember much else except the extensive bruising which was left as a result. I was fifteen. Why could my life not be normal? Why did walking with two boys to a display where half the school would have been in attendance warrant a beating? It served as another reminder of how awful life was at home.

There was a huge wardrobe in my bedroom that not only held the clothes but had plenty of room to sit at the bottom and hide. That was the place I chose to hide my 'run away' bag. My plan was that if an opportune moment came, I would leave and camp out under hedges - yes hedges! I had thought it through, and this seemed the best option as no money was required. A few jumpers and jeans for a change and the all-important custard cream biscuits wrapped up in tin-foil.

There was plenty of bamboo canes in the garage that I could loop the handles of the bag through and put it over my shoulder to carry it.

The bag never got used but it was there for years - just in case.

Throughout that period in my life, I remember asking God to take us away from Dad and bring Mum back or let us go and live with my aunt. Anywhere, as long as it was far away from the house, the anger, the beatings, the fear. Yet even as children we knew that if it was reported to the police then we would end up separated and in care. We stuck together - the three musketeers.

Then the questions came – why would God would allow this to happen? After all, as a child of God (I had got saved at age 12), surely He would have protected me and stopped this? There were so many times that I sat and cried, begging God to do something - but nothing. Why was He not listening?

Why did family not intervene? Did they realise the full extent of what was going on? If they did why do they choose to ignore it?

I had all of these questions but very few answers until years later when my aunt told my sister that we hid what it was like at home really well. They had an idea of some things, but there was a threat that loomed over them that if they intervened then they would never get to see us again. I can only imagine the impact that would have had on them.

Finally, I had a way out - an escape - and I was most certainly going to take it. I applied for nurse training which would mean living in the nurse's home. It was perfect – it covered all the basics of somewhere to live, studying but working and being paid and in three years qualifying as a nurse.

The day came with my belongings packed into the car and off we went. There were no goodbyes or well wishes. Here I was leaving home and it was my aunt which took me. Dad stayed at home.

Being a parent, I find it inconceivable that I would let my children begin a new chapter in their lives and not be a part of it. In stark contrast to my own life when my eldest daughter left for university the car was crammed packed and the journey began with a 7am sailing. A six-hour drive followed, then the unpacking and a day spent in the city where she was studying until finally the goodbyes had to be said and I was leaving my baby.

I am in no doubt that she was delighted to have that freedom just as I was the day that I left home at seventeen. For her it was adventure though, with a new city and new people, while for me it was freedom from a tyrant.

Many years later a woman prayed with me (without knowing my background), and as she prayed, she looked at me and said, 'God did not do this to you - it was the enemy. God was with you the whole time. He never left your side'.

That's the only thing that I can say for certain about this stage in my life. I knew that God was with me because I only survived those years because of His grace and strength. I had learnt the lesson that God never leaves me and never will, but there was still the negative impact it had on my life. When people were speaking about the love of the Father only wanting the best for us as His children I just couldn't relate because of my own experience. It took years before that revelation became real to me and destroyed the belief which I had held for so long.

Yet I would soon find myself walking a road where there was no room for doubt - that despite my childhood - would I completely trust God to see me through?

Hope in the Valley

Chapter 2

THE WHITE ROOM

I had a plan. I lay staring in disbelief at the oxygen monitor on my finger. The flashing blue digits were showing the number 71%.

Surely that wasn't right - maybe the monitor was faulty.

I proceeded to put the monitor on different fingers of both hands only to be disappointed in the results of 71-73%. There was no escaping the fact that this monitor was working and accurately at that.

Over twenty years ago I had developed a specialist interest in respiratory conditions and that had become the main focus of my job. I knew what these figures meant.

I needed to act and act fast.

I needed a plan.

In my head I quickly devised it: -.

I would ring the on-call doctors (it was a weekend).

Go to hospital ONLY if they suggested it.

Receive the required treatment (thinking antibiotics and oxygen).

Be home within 5-7days. Perfect.

Feeling rather pleased with myself I lifted the phone and dialled the number. The call handler was given the necessary information and advised me that a doctor would ring back. All I had to do was lie down again and wait – no sooner had the call ended when the phone buzzed beside me.

I found it difficult answering the doctors list of questions as I was becoming even more breathless. I found myself saying a few words, then stop for a break before continuing with the consultation. The doctor politely listened while I put forward my suggestion that I probably needed antibiotics and other medication. Unsurprisingly, he decided that this was not the best plan considering the circumstances and that the only option would be to go straight to hospital in an ambulance.

An ambulance?? Did he not know that the street I lived on was extremely small and that all the neighbours would see it and me being taken out to it? Could ambulances not have a stealth mode option that could be used before they turn into the street and park at the door?

The White Room

Meanwhile I went about waiting for the ambulance. Firstly, I had to get showered and dressed. After all I couldn't attend the hospital without ensuring that I was clean and well presented. By the time I had pulled myself up to sit at the end of the bed I gave in. Concentrating on my breathing, I tried regulating it with breathing exercises but it was no good. Small quick breaths were all I could manage and I had to enlist the help of my family.

Secondly, there was the short walk to the living room in this state. With legs like jelly, I held onto my husband and slowly walked to the recliner chair and flopped into it. It was exhausting sitting, with what felt like a tonne of bricks sitting on my chest Every minute that went by struggling for breath seemed liked a lifetime.

All I could do was pray that the ambulance would soon arrive and that my lungs would keep working. After a bit of a wait the ambulance arrived – it certainly didn't have stealth mode – with blue lights flashing it drove into the street before coming to a standstill at the entrance of the driveway.

The paramedics worked quickly, attaching me to oxygen and doing an assessment before getting me into the back of the ambulance. I looked out the circular window on the back door of the ambulance towards the house. My eldest daughter and husband were just standing, ashen faced, looking at the ambulance in disbelief – there was no time for hugs goodbye. All they could do was hand the paramedics my overnight bag and retreat.

And then we were off - enroute to the hospital.

Hope in the Valley

Chapter 3

HOPE IN HIS PRESENCE

I found myself alone in a room. I looked around at the white walls. The lighting was warm while almost dimmed - like the softer light that would be put in a bedroom. It gave the room a cosy feeling. But this wasn't a bedroom because there was no bed in the room.

Actually, there was nothing in this room - no furniture, pictures, window. Nothing to say that this room had been lived in.

I thought that if I went out of here then I could find someone who would be able to tell me where I was. At that moment it struck me - there was NO DOOR.

I was stuck in a room without a way out.

As a last resort I turned my attention to the ceiling, thinking that there would be a balcony to the left-hand side. There was nothing.

All of a sudden, I realised where I was and what was happening.

It was not like the movies at all!

I was in a coma.

This was NOT part of my plan.

Now that I was in a coma, I quickly discovered that films have definitely wrongly portrayed what it is like in the intensive care unit and how the recovery process unfolds. They generally portray a light at the end of the tunnel or an out of body experience with the person waking up and having an uneventful recovery.

I remembered being told the account of my mum's experience before she died of cancer. Apparently, she was in a tunnel with a light and she saw Jesus. I always loved that story of Jesus just waiting for her and its why I have grown up not fearing death. Knowing that Mum loved the Lord and was in heaven meant that I knew when my time came, He would be there waiting for me.

I recall an elderly patient telling me about an out of body experience which had such a powerful effect on his life.

He had gone shopping with his wife and became unwell. Having already had a previous heart complaint he decided to get home before calling an ambulance. He recalled that he was watching the paramedics performing CPR on him and then he left the room and was transported to heaven. He described the sky being an intense blue with no clouds in the sky. Beneath his feet was vibrant green grass. Before he knew it, he was back in the living room, awake, with the paramedics telling him that they had lost him and he was lucky to be alive.

Weeping, this man kept asking me 'Why would God show me this?' I had such a sense from God that He wanted this gent to know how much He loved him. I replied, "Because He loves you".

When his wife died and went home to heaven a few weeks after this, he was comforted in knowing where she was and he could just see her in heaven enjoying the beauty. He possessed a peace that he would see her one day again.

Yet neither of these were my experiences.

For me there was no light at the end of a tunnel or out of body experience - I was just there.

I remember my eldest daughter asking me what it felt like and the only way I could describe it was that it was like being on a boat. My daughter had been talking to someone whose relative had been in a coma and they also thought that they were on a boat.

It was such a bizarre feeling. I was aware of activity on this boat - for example, patients arriving being wheeled on a trolley with two to three staff members. A red fabric bag was sitting on top of the white sheet at the end of the bed. Once the patient was handed over to the boat staff, the red bag was lifted and taken with those who had been responsible for the patient's transfer.

It must have been an emergency bag. I concluded that this boat was designed to take Covid patients from the nearby hospitals. The boat itself was docked not far from Belfast port with patients being transferred via helicopter onto deck. That way the hospitals could free up much-needed space for those not requiring intensive care.

Boat or not, I remained alone in the white room. As I stood looking around me, I felt an incredible sense of peace going through every part of my body and kept hearing the words "the peace of God which passes all understanding".

As those words bounced off the walls it seemed that every fibre of my being was bathed in peace - a peace so intense that nothing could shake it. Any doubts or fear were obliterated in its presence and I knew that this was a peace that only God Himself could give.

In my head I knew the verse in Isaiah 26:3 (NKJV) which says:

"You will keep him in perfect peace, whose mind is stayed on You because he trusts in You".

There it was - because he trusts in You. I had placed my trust in God years before as a twelve-year-old and received His free gift of salvation. A trust in Him which had been strengthened over the years throughout difficult times. He had never abandoned me or let me down.

I had a choice to make even now - would I trust Him in the middle of this?

Could I still hope for a good outcome even though my body was being viciously assaulted and battered by the enemy?

Looking back at notes on my phone, I can see God preparing me for this moment.

One of the days before the coma, I had been struggling with being stuck in bed, being attached to oxygen and having to get help from the nurse to get washed and use the commode at the bedside. Having to be reliant on others to help with intimate care was quite frankly embarrassing and left me feeling vulnerable. It's not as if I hadn't been a patient before, but never to this extent.

While I was grumbling to myself about it, the Lord was so good and patient. He reminded me that He himself had washed the feet of His disciples (John chapter 13:1-17). Peter was one of the disciples who was most uncomfortable with this and he protested, which I could definitely relate to at this particular moment.

As with Peter, the Lord responded to me. He knew my thoughts and that I was trying to resist the loss of independence. There was a gentleness and love in His voice as He tenderly whispered into my ear, 'Just let Me take care of you'. That whisper melted all the embarrassment I felt. He was wanting to help but I had to get me out of the way and my reliance on self and choose - would I give Him permission to help or would I continue to try and do this on my own?

It overwhelms me even now as I write that He is so gentle and He will not force anything on us. As soon as I made my decision to trust Him I wholeheartedly and unreservedly spoke four words aloud, 'Ok Lord, I trust You'.

At that moment it was as if I had just fallen backwards into His arms - strong arms - which He wrapped around me and which held me tight. In that embrace I felt safe and secure. I wasn't going through this by myself but God was holding me and He wasn't going to let go. He had taken away the embarrassment I felt and rubbed away at the self-reliance and with a grateful, humble heart I handed the reins over to Him.

I took one last look around the white room and again to where I thought the balcony would be. This was the all-important balcony where my family, who were already in heaven, would be standing waiting for my arrival.

I spoke the following words, not that anyone could hear them and they just bounced off the walls of the room anyway. But still, I said:

> *'Well Jesus isn't waiting for me and neither is my family, so it's not my time to go home to heaven'.*

I didn't know where I was going but I was about to find out.

Alone and unsure I found myself in uncharted territory.

There was no help, no-one to rescue me or to help me navigate my way through this place.

For the first time in my life, I was truly alone.

I didn't know what to do.

I tried to gather my thoughts.

I needed to get out of here.

I wanted to survive.

I could hear the words that I had read immediately before entering the white room:

> *"Have I not commanded you? Be strong and of good courage; do not be afraid, nor dismayed for the Lord your God is with you wherever you go."* (Joshua 1:9 NKJV).

By then I had already given my sister Gwyneth some instructions and when the medical team came over to place me in the coma I was completely at peace. How could I not be when God Himself had promised to be with me wherever I went?

Yet now I stood alone despite what the verse had said. Would His presence invade this empty space? My thoughts turned to a Bible story which had been regularly told to me as a child. It was of Jonah, a man who had been asked by God to carry out a specific assignment. Instead, Jonah went in the other direction and boarded a ship. During a violent storm Jonah was thrown overboard and God arranged for a great fish to swallow him.

I could picture Jonah inside this empty space - it was dark and slimy. It wasn't going to be a comfortable ride. There were no seats to sit on, food or light. Nevertheless, what it did provide was safety – a 'cocoon' from the dangers of the sea. No distractions – a place where he had plenty of time to reflect!

In the natural there was no point shouting for help, after all he was unreachable in the depths of the sea. The only person who knew where He was, was God Himself, the very One who he was running away from. Jonah quickly found out that there was no escape from the presence of the Lord. God was with him even in this inaccessible place.

The words of the Psalmist also make it very clear that we can never escape His presence.

> *"I can never escape from Your Spirit!*
> *I can never get away from Your presence!*
> *If I go up to heaven You are there*
> *If I go down to the grave, You are there"*
> Psalm 139:7-8 (NLT)

So why was I alone?

By now I was becoming agitated. Not only because of the situation but also because of the heat. There was no respite from the stifling heat. No trees to sit under to escape the intensity of the scorching sun's rays. It was uncomfortable, unbearable and there were no means to cool down.

I lifted my head but that was all I could move. I was stuck.

The crowds didn't make it any easier – they were all jostling, shouting, trying to out-do each other in order to get a better view. There was nothing that I could do to change where I was. The dry, dusty path ejected plumes of dust as the crowd went by which sent me into bouts of coughing.

The shouts, excited chatter and angry voices intensified as the footsteps quickened, causing the ground to vibrate beneath me. Fearing that I would be trampled on I tried in vain to pull myself up to see what all the commotion was about. I remained unnoticed among the multitudes, just an obstacle to avoid. Certainly, nobody seemed to notice my predicament and any attempts to speak was lost in the noise.

Suddenly, a hush descended over the place except for the sound of a loud voice shouting in desperation. The crowd had become like statues yet I could hear the noise of footsteps slowly approaching.

A sandalled foot appeared at my left-hand side.

I had such a strong urge to reach out and touch the person walking by, so I mustered up all of my strength in order to stretch out my arm. This person was close enough to help me in my predicament. Without even looking up, I knew who was approaching and I was adamant that this was an opportunity that I would not miss.

Jesus was walking by my side.

He was walking ever so slowly - every slow footstep intentional in its movement.

Yet He remained just out of arm's reach.

Everything else faded into the background and in that moment, it was me and Jesus, His presence pervading the atmosphere. His presence brought comfort into my situation. I was not forgotten by Him. He was there beside me.

This experience is as clear to me today as if it happened yesterday. I had just personally encountered the promise of Joshua chapter 1:9 and Psalm 139:7-8 for myself. An experience which is forever embedded in my heart. I am totally confident that no matter what challenges I face in the future, I will always have hope in His presence. He will do just as He promised and would remain by my side.

I had kept this experience to myself until a few months after getting home. My sister Gwyneth and I were having one of our many conversations. I told her what had happened and that it reminded me of the account of blind Bartimaeus in the Gospel of Mark.

Her response astonished me.

The following words are an excerpt from her prayer journal, dated on the first day of the coma:

> *"Picture of Jesus beside Hilary's bed in ICU, walking up and down by it, watching everything, never taking His eyes off her, His peace pervading that space, tangibly present"*

Chapter 4

THE LION ROARS

The stifling heat was replaced by a refreshing breeze - a very welcome relief to my body.

Gone was the flat dusty ground which I had just encountered and in its place were rolling hills with the scent of damp soil and vibrant green grass. In the distance was a dense clump of trees with mountain tops protruding above the tree line.

The smell of wood burning drifted through the air as a small fire crackled nearby which seemed to be much too small to serve the tents and shelters which were dotted around the area.

I could see hundreds and hundreds of people rushing around - in and out of the tents putting on armour in preparation for a battle. Some had almost chain-mail like tops, others were in ordinary clothes of red, green and blue, each one carrying swords which glistened in the sun.

Bravely they marched out from the confines of the camp onto the surrounding hills to take their positions.

I watched intrigued at what was unfolding before my eyes.

I had a sense of urgency to shout out, yet I was completely aware that I couldn't speak. It seemed pointless to even try because nobody would be able to hear me, yet the urgency intensified. This was something I just had to do. This was a moment of great magnitude - if I didn't do it then the consequences would be fatal.

I opened my mouth and shouted as loud as I could.

"VICTORY, VICTORY, VICTORY".

It felt as if these words were roaring from within me, bubbling up to the surface and increasing in intensity until I opened my mouth to speak. When I did no sound came out of my mouth, but I heard it within my spirit as loud and as plain as if I was speaking in the 'real' world.

I kept shouting louder and louder,

"VICTORY, VICTORY, VICTORY!".

Each word was more forceful than the last until, after what seemed to be an eternity, I could no longer sustain the strength to continue. I remember chuckling to myself and thinking that if anybody could see me, they would wonder what I was doing.

The Lion Roars

As it was, I knew that I was only being obedient to what the Holy Spirit was telling me to do. I am convinced that this shout of victory was a pivotal moment in my survival. There is absolutely no question in my mind that I was releasing my faith even while I was in the coma.

Suddenly, from nowhere, came the thunderous roar of a lion, which shook the ground and shook me to the core. This roar was unlike any other that I had ever heard. It was intense, fierce, powerful, victorious.

The army stood looking ahead, unfazed by the noise.

As the roar intensified, its sound reverberated to every corner of the earth. There was nowhere or no-one that did not hear this sound.

A declaration had been made throughout the earth.

Mesmerized, I watched as the lion walked past me. It's an image that I will never forget.

It was a picture of great strength - muscular, but graceful. The huge paws which caused a thud, created a tremor when they made contact with the ground. It's eyes glowed of shining amber, yet I wasn't afraid at the proximity of the lion. I felt safe yet in awe because I realised that this was no ordinary lion - this was the Lion of Judah - beautiful, majestic and conquering. Jesus, the Lion of Judah who had conquered sin and death for us was here in this battle.

It was at this point that a tall, thin metal stake with a flag was pushed into the ground. The red flag billowed in the wind showing the crest of a golden lion visible for all to see. This ground was protected and no enemy or force could stand in this place - It had to flee!

I heard in my spirit that *'the victory has been decreed over the land'*.

This was the moment that the official order for my victory had been declared.

It may seem bizarre that I could shout and release faith while in a coma – all I know is that in the natural when the Holy Spirit prompts you to say something that it will line up with the Bible. I know that by being obedient, I was partnering with Him. There is a verse in the Bible which says:

> *"For whatever is born of God overcomes the world*
> *And this is the victory that has overcome the world - our faith".*
> 1 John5:4-6 (NKJV)

Unbeknownst to me, an intense battle was raging for my life. My body was being ravaged by the attack of the enemy with low blood pressure, oxygen levels and kidneys being affected, only to name a few issues.

My body had picked up another infection and it was proving very difficult to treat despite being on six antibiotics. Any treatment was proving unsuccessful. As a last resort the microbiology consultant came into ICU to see. The staff were given the arduous task of removing and replacing all the lines and tubes which were inserted into my body - lines for drips, arterial line for measuring blood gases, tube in nose into my stomach, even lines in my feet!

Now all they could do was watch and wait.

The battle raged on each day, bringing its own challenges, but eventually about a month into the coma a very small window of opportunity had opened allowing for a much-needed CT scan. Even though I was still deemed seriously ill, the scan was imperative to rule out clots in the lungs. Flanked by a full medical team, I was wheeled quickly down to the scanner before returning to ICU staff who eagerly awaited the results - as were my family.

On admission to hospital, I had nominated my eldest daughter, Judith and my twin sister, Gwyneth, to be the contacts for the medical team. They were then to relay all medical information to my husband in layman terms so that he would understand what was going on (he and I had agreed to this when I was first admitted). As a nurse my sister would know the specific questions to ask, while my daughter, a law student, had a talent for gaining all the necessary information with questioning, processing it and asking more questions!

No-one in the family was prepared for this journey or the difficult conversations which had to take place with the medical team.

When I awoke from the coma, the first doctor who spoke informed me that I had been very ill. Of course, he did not elaborate which did not suit my nurse's head at all. I wanted to know how ill, although with the serious look on his face and reluctance to elaborate I could guess. I decided to help him out in this by asking on what scale of 'very ill' had I been. The 'not very ill', 'ill' or 'critically ill that family had to be called' was the gauge.

Pausing after saying each one I waited for a response. Nothing. Until the last one was reached, and he nodded. He looked a bit relieved that I didn't have much of a reaction. There was no point because his first few words had indicated the gravity of the situation. He certainly didn't give away any details, so it was left to me to interrogate my sister Gwyneth and daughter Judith. I was shocked when I heard what they had to say. It all seemed surreal.

On not one but five occasions, Gwyneth and Judith nervously answered calls from the medical team. The conversations were matter of fact - my life was holding on by a very fine thread and they were progressing to provide end of life care.

A "do not resuscitate" order had been placed over my life which meant that if there was any deterioration in my heart, the medical team would not actively respond. This I think was probably the worst part of the journey to realise that the medical team had deemed my condition to be terminal. Hope was fading and fast. The doctors were monitoring my condition hour by hour but this changed to minute by minute as my condition deteriorated.

On two occasions Gwyneth and Judith sat in the sterile relative's room and listened to the doctors who had been monitoring my condition on an hourly basis. Now, as my health deteriorated further, the monitoring became minute to minute - each minute possibly my last. Refusing to believe that this would happen, Gwyneth and Judith relayed their appreciation to all the staff but informed them that I was a woman of faith and that the family were praying for a miracle.

Family, friends, my Pastor, church family and people unknown in churches across Northern Ireland, the UK, America and Canada were praying for me. People who I had never met were coming together to pray for a touch from God, a miracle, a stand of faith in what God could do and that it would happen.

It didn't stop there - I was getting the Word of God into my spirit. No visitors were allowed into ICU because of Covid restrictions so video calls were made available for relatives to stay in contact with their loved ones.

Faithfully, Judith used these daily calls to play worship songs or teachings from ministers who she knew I listened to. The nurses would often set the iPad on my pillow and let it play. She would also read Psalm 91 to me - a Psalm which she knew that I read and prayed over my life on a daily basis. Each verse was filled with the promises of God but now the last two verses of that chapter were crucial:

> *"He shall call upon me and I will answer him,*
> *I will be with him in trouble,*
> *I will deliver and honour him.*
> *With long life I will satisfy him,*
> *And show him My salvation"*
> (Psalm 91:15&16, NKJV)

Meanwhile Judith was keeping a record of what they were believing for and another list of answered prayed.

Her 'believing for' list included:

Oxygen weaning successfully within 24hours – target of 30% oxygen.

Successful, spontaneous breathing trial.

Successful extubating and no CPAP required after extubating.

Peaceful spirit.

Reduced inflammation levels.

Bowel had stopped working - start working again.

Her answered prayer list included:

Inflammation levels (CRP) reduced - was 500 on the Sunday and by Thursday it was 20.

Temperature 40 degrees on Sunday - completely gone by Tuesday.

Oxygen requirement reduced from 100% to 50% and maintained.

The Lion Roars

All organs working completely without any support – bowel wasn't working on Sunday night with significant improvements by Wednesday morning.

The victory which had been decreed was taking place.

Hope in the Valley

Chapter 5

TIME

I felt like a fish in a goldfish bowl. My two eyes were looking at the outside world, only to see seven sets of eyes looking back at me. I wanted them to go. There was nowhere for me to hide. I felt awkward sitting in bed, in the mandatory hospital gown with a thin sheet for cover, as they conversed about my medical journey thus far.

The physiotherapist must have noticed the horrified look on my face. Quickly she moved to the bottom of the bed and as she swished the blue curtains together, she told the doctors that 'all would be revealed in a moment'.

The two of us dissolved into stifled giggles, especially at the look on their faces.

I was nervous. What if it didn't work or I wasn't able to manage it? This step was something I was looking forward too, something that the physiotherapist had talked about for the past week.

She placed a small round box on the table in front of me and inside was an object like an old wooden thread spool. There were two differences - firstly it was made of green plastic and secondly it was marginally smaller in diameter.

I eyeballed that spool and was determined that this would be easily inserted into my throat. It had too.

Before being ventilated I hadn't even considered what my recovery would look like as I had never worked in an intensive care setting or knew anybody personally who had been in a coma. It was a huge blow to discover that the road to recovery would be extremely steep due to the devastating consequences of the coma.

The greatest shock for me at this time was the discovery that a tracheostomy (a hole in the front of my neck into the windpipe) had been inserted to help with breathing while I was in the coma. This meant that I couldn't speak at all. It was frightening. My only contact with a tracheostomy prior to this was as a student nurse. A particular, middle-aged gentleman had a tracheostomy which blocked regularly and had other issues. I vividly remember him as we tried to clear the blockages. Was this what I would now be faced with?

Time

Every twelve hours like clockwork the tube had to be changed and it was hateful. The oxygen had to be disconnected as the tube was taken out to be cleaned and then it was quickly replaced by another. I would lie there and pray that it would be quick and easy because at times it was difficult to get it back into position. As soon as I would hear the click, I would breathe a sigh of relief.

However, the times when it was proving difficult to click into position was horrendous. Every second felt like a lifetime until it was connected and the flow of oxygen reached my airways once again. What would happen if it couldn't be changed? How long could I last without the oxygen being disconnected? Would I come through a coma only to lose my life to a tube being changed? These thoughts tried to run riot in my mind and it took every ounce of my being to fight the thoughts with God's Word and to trust Him completely.

Everyday brought on new challenges, but not being able to speak and communicate with the staff was the worst at this present time. To try and help me, a nurse brought pen and paper over so that I could write what I needed. Unfortunately, this wasn't a viable option as I wasn't able to hold or grip the pen, let alone write.

The only way left to communicate was to try and point to things or mouth the words. It was like a game of charades, with staff trying to guess what I wanted - a game I had always disliked - even more so now as this was now my reality. When one nurse couldn't understand, she would bring over another colleague and another until somebody was able to decipher the gestures. Thankfully there were a few who were clearly skilled at charades and were able to interpret quite quickly.

I felt so isolated, frustrated and occasionally scared. These feelings escalated during the night because I couldn't sleep and there were slightly less staff on duty. Staff would walk past my bed or be sitting watching the monitor about a foot from the bottom of the bed. I had no way to call for help if I needed it, especially as part of a pillar obscured my view. It wasn't enough to try and make eye contact. I needed to be able to tell them if I needed suctioning or if my breathing felt worse. One staff member suggested that I could rattle the bed rails which were kept up. This idea slightly helped, but the majority of the time I hadn't the strength to grip the rails. The staff then told the next shift to listen out for the rattling bars. This worked. Now when staff passed by, they would ask if I needed anything.

I needed my speech back!

I looked at the valve again and gave the physiotherapist 'the nod'.

It was time - within seconds the valve was in and I opened my mouth.

For the first time in two months, I spoke!

The physiotherapist hugged and jumped about excitedly.

I cried at the sound of my own, shaky voice.

Time

The curtains were pulled back to the applause of those standing by.

We were so excited that the physiotherapist said I had to ring one of the family so that they could hear me talk again. At this stage I couldn't even hold my phone, let alone dial – but she did it for me. From what I remember she had a chat with them as well! Her sincerity, enthusiasm and compassion are something that I will always remember.

This was the first milestone in my recovery and it felt good, however was no time for rest. I had to keep going. In my head there was a checklist which needed to be completed. The next on the list was the suction which had to be done to help remove any build-up of mucus from my chest. It was hateful!

The only way I could describe it is that when the suction tube was inserted into the hole in my throat, it felt as though hundreds of razors blades were rubbing against each other deep in my chest. It brought tears to my eyes every time and honestly if I could have moved, I would have run out of that place at the very mention of suction. As the need for suction lessened, I used to shake my head and mouth the words 'I hate this' to them. Finally, the day came when the tube was removed and the open wound at my throat was being left to heal over.

Goodbye suction!!

Those early days of waking up could be summed up as a catalogue list of loss which just seemed to be mounting up. With the doctors not being optimistic that I would achieve a full recovery, they focused on the loss of movement. Every time a doctor came over to me, I knew the routine - move fingers and toes and squeeze their fingers with my fingers. It was their measuring tool which they used many times in a day.

In all honesty I didn't understand the concern - at this point I was unaware of the prognosis which they had given to my family. It was only later that my daughter revealed that the doctors had reported that although I was awake and responsive, I was unable to wiggle my toes and barely able to lift my fingers. They explained that this may not improve.

I can't even begin to put into words how I felt then. Negative thoughts were trying to run rampant in my head. 'What if' scenarios were starting to play in slow motion, but every time they did, I had to be determined to believe the promises of God. God brought me from the brink of death and I firmly believed that He wasn't going to leave me as I was, lying in a hospital bed. His report was better. His report was that there was a plan and a future for me, that He had healed all of my diseases and that He was the restorer of my life. I had to trust Him.

It didn't stop me from staring intensely at my feet as I tried to wiggle them, willing them to move, as if my staring was going to jolt them into action, but to no avail. I would be hoping against hope that the next time the doctors came past and asked, that there would be a glimmer of movement. What would happen if I wasn't able to walk again and stuck in a wheelchair the rest of my life? I lost count of the 'Jesus help me' prayers that were said during this time. I would smile, thinking to myself about those prayers. Every one of them answered. It didn't mean that I didn't have to go through it. I did, but that's the thing - I did get through it with Gods help.

There is a verse in 2 Corinthians chapter 12:9 which I clung to at that time:

"And He said to me, My grace is sufficient for you, for My strength is made perfect in weakness".

There was so much that had been lost during the past two months. I still couldn't get my head around the fact that it was now a few days away from the end of September.

The plans of the summer had disintegrated with my hospital admission - a family girls' night away, another night away with my sister and the random road trips which we would do. Although this was lost it didn't concern me as much as I knew that we would re-book it again in the future, whatever that future would look like.

Some special family birthdays had been and gone, but what upset me the most at this time was not being there to take my youngest to collect her GCSE exam results. It was a tradition in our family that on GCSE results day, all the girls in the family went out, usually for breakfast or brunch. Instead, my sister had jumped into the role while I had to be patient and wait for my sister to hear the results. On the positive side there was nothing wrong with my hearing!

Lying in hospital provided ample opportunity to mull over the time which had been lost, not only in these short few months but over a life-time.

How much time over the years had been squandered?

Time lost is never regained.

There was nothing that could be done to rewind and have a second chance. There was only one thing to do - go forward with a fresh perspective on how precious time is and how to wisely spend that time.

While I was in the coma, I heard the words, 'Only one life it will soon be past, only what's done for Jesus will last'. I sensed that there was an urgency in these words because life goes by so quickly and every moment of time was precious. It was time to focus on those things which would last for eternity, rather than focusing on things which could be lost in an instance.

> *"Whereas you do not know what will happen tomorrow. For what is your life? It is even a vapour, that appeared for a little time and then vanisheth away".* (James 4:14 NKJV).

This verse had even more revelation to me now than it had as a child of twelve years of age giving their life to Jesus. The last two months of my life had shown that we don't know what is going to happen the next day, let alone the hour or minute. It only takes a second for life to change and to be in the clutches of death.

Time

These thoughts and verse were very fresh in my mind and had been occupying my thinking when I found myself in a sticky situation one particular night. My sister had been asked by doctors to encourage me to lie on my stomach which would help to expand the lungs and in turn would help my breathing. As her texts came through, I remember telling her, as I did to doctors, that I couldn't lie on my stomach. However, I knew to appease everybody I would need to give it a go.

The night staff came on duty and just before midnight they came over to help reposition me to lie on my stomach. As soon as they got me turned over my breathing became a lot worse and I was struggling. The only way to describe it was as if a pillow had been put over my nose and mouth and I remember trying unsuccessfully to move myself. Everything around me was starting to fade into the distance and I looked up at the monitor and saw that the oxygen levels were at 21%! A yell went from a nurse to "Get a doctor, any doctor!" and I could hear the noise of feet running.

"Jesus help me," was all I could say in my head before it all went black. I don't know how long it was before I opened my eyes and a nurse was standing beside me, smiling, telling me that I had given them all a shock. I smiled back. Life is definitely unpredictable!

I stood in that white room. I repented for the lost opportunities and the time which had been wasted over the years. Now it was time to evaluate what had I done for Jesus.

Hope in the Valley

What did I need to change? Now was a time for me to move forward and ensure my life would count for Jesus and for eternity.

What about your life?

If your life changed within the next second - what would it look like?

Do you know Jesus? If you already do, then how are you spending your time?

Time lost is never regained.

Chapter 6

THE VICTORY CLAP

It was a hectic Monday on the ward, even busier than usual. The doctors were doing their rounds, patients were getting washed and enabled to sit up if they could, while others were having their daily physiotherapy. Multiple amounts of trolleys and beds were being pushed in the corridor and past my bed. There was activity everywhere.

In contrast my morning was quiet. Nobody had come round to wash me and get me out to sit on the chair nor had the physiotherapists appeared to release their torture. I spent my morning dozing and proceeded to do the same in the afternoon. Closing my eyes and trying to block out the noise, I fell asleep. I felt a bump. Whatever it was it jolted me awake. I opened my eyes to discover two nurses at the side of my bed smiling down at me. (This was never a sign of good news).

Despite their smiles they had a look of sheer determination on their faces. They proposed a bed-bath alongside getting my hair washed. Getting my hair washed was quite a palaver. Do you know how difficult it is to get hair washed while lying flat in bed? They had come prepared. The trolley was wheeled in from behind the curtain and before I knew it, I had been scrubbed, washed, dried and moisturised. Finally, I was left alone, lying back with my head on the soft plumped-up pillows. I closed my eyes and the noise of the ward faded into the distant as I began to drift off.

I was disturbed again.

This time it was to discuss the NG tube that went up my nose and into the stomach. The nostril with the tube had become very painful – it was stinging and burning constantly. I hadn't mentioned it before because it seemed so ridiculous that in the middle of a critical care unit I was complaining of a sore nostril. I couldn't endure the pain it any longer however, so when the nurses were washing me, I told them about it. Gently they removed a corner of the tape and found that a small sore had developed.

After a bit of a discussion the rest of the tape was pulled off - they had decided to remove the tube. This tube had been in the whole time I had been in a coma so that I could be fed straight into my stomach and receive all of my medication. In all

The Victory Clap

seriousness, I asked if it was going to hurt and could it wait. I really didn't like the thought of it being removed because the nostril was too sore. I was also a bit squeamish at the thought of the sensation of it being pulled out from my nose which really bothered me. Without any time to think or protest though, the tube was quickly pulled out and dangling in front of me, leaving me in a spasm of coughing but relieved that it was over in the matter of seconds!

What a day this had turned out to be - bed bathed, hair washed, the numerous IV lines had also been removed and now the NG tube. Where on earth would it end??

A few hours later I would find out.

In my head I was already trying to think of which staff would be in that night when the phone rang at the nurses' station. I caught a glimpse of the nurse looking over at me while she was talking and of course being a nurse, my curiosity began to get the better of me. One of the things I had noticed over my time here was that if a nurse was on the phone talking about you, they usually looked over at you. I often wondered if that is something that I have done in the past. This nurse was definitely looking over at me during her conversation. Before long she came over and said that a bed was available on a ward. I had been told a few days prior to this that I was fit to return to the ward for the next stage of care. I just didn't know when that would be.

I started crying - something I hadn't done until now.

The nurse looked a bit startled and thought I needed a pep talk which I didn't. In that moment I was overwhelmed with Gods love, power and faithfulness. Suddenly and against all odds, I was leaving the intensive care unit. In the natural I should have died.

BUT my God.

And today marked that victory.

It was daunting to be leaving the ICU and going to a ward which would not have the same staff-to-patient ratio. I asked God to send me to a ward that was used to dealing with patients like myself because at present I required help for everything. I just hoped that it wouldn't be in a care of the elderly ward. At least I was able to talk again which would help enormously, but it didn't stop my mind running riot and thinking of worse case scenarios. What would happen if my breathing got worse or if I needed to be re-positioned in bed? What if the staff didn't come in quickly enough?

Fear and worry were trying to take hold. God had preserved my life yet these thoughts came flooding in. I had to stop this and quick.

The Bible says that we are to cast down arguments which do not line up with the Word of God. (Paraphrased from 2 Corinthians 10:5). I had to get my thoughts on what God said and not let fear and worry run rampant. I knew the importance of recognising fear and worry and the negative impact it can have on your life. It can start that downward spiral causing sleeplessness, panic attacks, low mood or depression.

I realise that this is a huge battle for people, and this is by no means undermining mental health challenges. As a believer I had the solution available. I had to overcome these thoughts so that they wouldn't take root in my thinking and hamper my recovery. I did what I knew to do - I went over scripture which reaffirmed that God was with me, that He is good and to give all my concerns over to God.

The solution verse I used was Phillipians 4:6-7 (NLT). "Don't worry about anything; instead, pray about everything. Tell God what you need and thank Him for ALL He has done. THEN you will experience God's peace, which exceeds anything we can understand. His peace will guard your hearts and minds as you live in Christ Jesus".

I had the solution - I just had to apply it.

So, with every problem and scenario that my head could possibly conceive, I followed the instructions in Phillipians. Once I had handed it over to God, there was no taking it back again. Yet the enemy still tried. I would reply aloud, "No, I've given it to God and I'm not worrying about it" or "No, God says not to let my heart be troubled, but to trust in Him" (John14:1 NLT).

I had to stand strong. I had to resist these thoughts with the Word until they stopped, which they did, because the Word of God works. His Word is the weapon which will bring down and defeat the attacks the enemy tries to bring against us but only if we don't give up.

That peace did come over me - I was ready to go.

As I left ICU, the staff stood at the sides of the corridor and applauded me – a clap of honour. To me it was a clap of victory – victory that was only possible through Jesus Christ.

I wondered how many times the staff had been able to do this over the past two years. How many families were able to be re-united with their loved ones on a ward just as mine would be? Certainly, the fifty-four days which I had spent with them seemed to be a significant amount of time to have this moment.

God had brought me through the valley of the shadow of death. He was my Hope in that valley and He would continue to be my Hope in the next stage of my journey.

Chapter 7

HELLO LAZARUS

"Hello Lazarus".

There couldn't have been a more suitable greeting.

Gwyneth, my sister, had arrived and was bustling about the room when her mobile phone rang.

'Look who I have here!' she exclaimed as she swung the phone round in front of me.

Looking back was my older brother Graeme, looking pleased at himself because of his droll greeting. Of course it didn't help that Gwyneth and I erupted into laughter. Big brother was checking up to make sure the updates that he was receiving were accurate. Now I was awake to verify in person that all was okay. He was obviously satisfied as the call was over quickly.

It made my night being able to see another family member again even though it was over a video call.

I had missed them.

When I was first admitted, it felt like solitary confinement. That changed as I left the confines of ICU, with their doors swinging shut behind me and being wheeled to the ward. It was almost leisurely, with the staff chatting as we meandered through the corridors until I was brought to a standstill in a single room.

Another ward, another room, another set of staff to get used to. Well, not exactly - remember the prayer in the previous chapter? Well God answered that prayer. I was back in the same ward where I had been admitted to, just in a different room number.

I was told by staff that throughout my time in ICU they had continued to keep up to date on my progress. When it was time for me to be moved onto a ward, they said that they would take me back. Even while typing this, I am so grateful to God for this because it may seem such a minor detail but to me it was everything. It was familiar and I had confidence in the staff who would now be seeing me through this next stage.

The first thing I noticed about the ward was the darkness outside. It was only eight o'clock at night yet here I was looking around me in the dimly lit room. The blinds on the corridor window were opened which meant I could look out and watch people scurrying about. At some point I must have dozed off, only to be woken by the sound of the door opening.

Two people entered the room wearing masks, visors and aprons. I had not initially realised it, but to my absolute amazement behind those masks in waltzed my sister and daughter!! They looked extremely pleased with themselves at gaining entry to my room and with lots of giggling, relayed how they had obtained permission to get in to see me.

When the family had had been informed of the move it was decided that my sister, Gwyneth and eldest daughter Judith would be the two designated visitors while I was on the ward. Mainly due to the fact that they had been liaising with the medical staff throughout. The staff had kindly agreed to their pleading that they could have a very quick visit that night.

This was the first time we had seen each other in person since I had left the ward. And they were here right in front of me!

I think I can safely say that we were all grinning like Cheshire cats. There was so much excited chatter, mostly from them, because I was too tired. I was more than happy to listen. Just to have them at my bedside and know that they would be able to visit every day meant everything. It would help make the arduous road to recovery a lot easier. Before I knew it, they were back out the door with a flurry of waves and plans to visit the next day.

Settling down and anticipating a quiet night's sleep, I lay back on the starched white pillows and smiled. My heart was full of gratitude to God. To me this was His doing. He knew exactly what I needed at that time and it happened. That visit was what we all had prayed, hoped and believed would happen and my God didn't disappoint.

The journey was not over yet and I knew that there were still many obstacles to overcome but that was for tomorrow. Tonight, I was going to sleep, content in the knowledge that I was progressing.

I would love to be able to say that the night passed off without incident, but unfortunately that was not the case.

In the early hours of the morning, I was struggling with chest pain.

My mind was racing.

Was I having a heart attack?

An asthma attack?

Would I have to go back to ICU?

That was a thought I couldn't even entertain.

Deep breaths Hilary.

I lay waiting for the symptoms to ease.

I prayed.

Then waited.

I placed my finger on the nurse call button which had been attached to the sheet.

Then I realised that I had not had a nebuliser (a way of getting the medication to open the airways instead of inhalers).

When the nurse arrived, I calmly asked for a nebuliser. This was not as simple as I had hoped. Looking horrified, I explained to the nurse that I was not having a heart attack but this was asthma related. Before I knew it the ECG machine was wheeled in and the doctors were waiting for the results. Finally with the doctors happy that this was not a heart attack, I had the nebuliser and fell asleep only to be woken up again with the clattering of the bin in the room.

It was 5.30am! A new routine had begun.

The best part of all was that every day I had two giggling visitors, always looking pleased with themselves and who knew more about my care than I did. If they didn't know it - it wasn't worth knowing.

They would come in laughing at the hill they had to walk up to get to the hospital, what level they had got parked on and how it had boosted their count of steps for the day. I don't think they ever saw an improvement with their fitness levels with that cardio workout. It was a daily challenge. Although I did mention that I thought it was good of me to provide them with this opportunity to help maintain their physical activity, only to be met with rolling eyes and groans.

Hope in the Valley

As much as I loved the visits, I tried to convince them that a twice-weekly visit would be enough. My protests were to fall on deaf ears. They reasoned that they had earned the right to daily visits after all I had put them through. They had a point! There was no reply to that! The visits continued and were always appreciated.

At this point it was two months since I had last seen my husband Mark and youngest daughter Sophie in person. There was a brief video call with all the family before I had gone to ICU with Mark present. I saw his lip quivering as he struggled to maintain his composure, but it was too overwhelming. He said "Hello" and then had to leave the room. He had been there in the background, struggling to comes to terms with the reality of the situation, being a dad to Sophie and working what hours he could.

I had been on the ward just over a week when Mark came to visit me in hospital with Judith. I was so happy to see him but at the same time I was concerned of how he would react. His wife, stuck in a bed, with a glaringly obvious purple/red wound at her throat and various other tubes. Would he cope?

The first thing I noticed about him was the shirt he was dressed in and the smell of his aftershave. His strong bear hug melted away all my concerns. He pulled a chair up and sat holding my hand through the bed guard rail, talking or just sitting smiling. Whatever the future held, he was going to be there.

Finally, I saw Sophie – well via a video call at least. With being on a Covid ward it was not somewhere I wanted her to be just to visit me. The video calls were enough until I got home, catching up on what was going on with the dogs being brought into the camera view too. On the odd occasion the rabbit attended the video calls too. While I had been away, she had cut her hair short, tried out new recipes and had her dad as chief tester. He had two options in her eyes - eat it or try and cook yourself. Not being a gourmet chef, my husband's repertoire was beans, pizza or cereal!

Throughout the day the rest of the family kept in contact over our family chat group. All of this helped to pass the days in the ward.

As a nurse I knew that there were benefits for patients to receive visitors. I was now on the other side of nursing literature and the various research which had been carried out in this area of patient care. One of the main benefits would be that it improves patients' emotional wellbeing and assists in their recovery.

From a patient perspective I have found this to be true. Every day I looked forward to the visits. It provided something to look forward to, family, (Gwyneth and Judith) could see how I actually was and often they would stop at the nurse's station to raise any queries before leaving.

There was always something to laugh about and yet if I was not having such a good day, they were my encouragers. They were the voice of reason, the "don't be so hard on yourself, look at what you have gone through, it will take time" encouraging voices in my ear.

Time – the word that started the multitude of questions – how much time? Is it time to go home? When will I get home? How long before I can lift a spoon and feed myself or be able to lift a tumbler to drink water? Most importantly was the question, "How long before I could walk again?" I wanted to fast-forward to the time when all the effects of this illness had completely disappeared.

It was a question which I asked time and time again, but obviously the medical and nursing staff were unable to give timeframes which was frustrating as a patient, even though I understood why. Any conversation was directed at the next step rather than the long term, yet I felt I needed to hear the long term. Did they expect full recovery or was I going to be left requiring care for the rest of my life?

These are only some of the thoughts that went through my mind, yet I knew that regardless of any negative outlook that would be made that I would be determined and stand in faith to prove that my God was greater than the problem. After all, God had brought me this far and I was expecting a full recovery even though it was going to be a process and take time.

The Lord reminded me through the words in Matthew's gospel chapter 6, that I focus on the day at hand - the now, rather than look at the bigger picture and all that needed to be achieved to get home. I relied on His strength to get me through every challenge I faced and He didn't disappoint.

The exhaustion was indescribable – no amount of sleep seemed to improve it. I felt lazy sleeping all the time and very frustrated. It didn't matter who talked reason to me - I wanted to feel energetic again and to be less dependent on people for even the most menial tasks. My body however required the opposite and I realised that by not resting I would be hindering the process of recovery.

I did what I knew to do -I spoke out Bible verses which spoke of healing and strength. I listened to podcasts of different ministers, played worship music and at night an audio Bible was set to play. I was surrounding myself with the Word of God and as I did, I knew that it would be doing its work of encouraging, strengthening and transforming me.

Every day I made the decision to be positive and tackle every obstacle head on. One of my sayings in life when trials come is that 'I refuse to quit'. With that tenacity and a hope and trust in God I decided that no matter how hard the recovery would be I would achieve the goal of walking again, of getting home and live life to the full but most importantly a life for Jesus.

"Only one life it will soon be past, only what's done for Jesus will last"

These are words which I had heard clearly while I was in the coma. It was a familiar saying which I had heard throughout my life but now it took on a new perspective in light of what I had just been through. With having experienced the fragility of life I had plenty of time lying in hospital to re-evaluate my priorities to ensure that Jesus was at the centre of my life. Was there anything that was out of balance? Was I being led by the Holy Spirit or was I being led by my own desires and wants?

All of these questions and many more were brought to God and His reply was, "One day at a time."

He had the answers and knew my heart but for now it was taking each day as it comes. There was enough grace and strength for those 24 hours with its ward routine, the occupational therapy, the speech and language therapy, the exercises – there was certainly enough to focus on for now. Any adjustments needed in my life would come but until that time it was God and I in that room together. The One who never left my side, the One who knew how I felt and the One who gave me His love, compassion and strength to keep me going.

Chapter 8

IT'S OK TO CRY

Having faith doesn't mean that a believer cannot cry. Instead, it means that despite the tears which are falling, faith says that we will overcome and see the victory.

My sister Gwyneth told me of an incident while I was writing this book and I must admit it tugged on my heart strings. I felt the deep anguish of my family as she spoke.

I was still in the coma.

My eyes began fluttering, at the sound of the voices and a solitary tear rolled slowly from my eye and made its way down my cheek.

The daily video calls which the ward staff arranged so that my family could speak to me, continued. As mentioned in a previous chapter, my daughter Judith had decided that she would use this time talking to me, playing worship music, reading Psalm 91 and other chapters of the Bible.

Today was different - there was another voice - the voice of one who had been with me throughout my life - my twin. It's said by family that without speaking a word but with various glances we can have a full conversation in a room full of people - and we can. There have been times when we just know that the other one is in trouble or feeling unwell. It is definitely a twin thing.

As Judith was speaking and saying 'Look who is here, come on Mum you're doing great', Gwyneth, my twin sister then spoke. At that moment there was movement - much to the consternation of Judith - who declared, 'Well I don't get a response like that'.

One small solitary tear was enough to give hope to them that day that I could hear them. I may have been 'lost' but I was listening to them and now there was a glimmer of hope. I was in there. I had responded.

That tear was the first of a few to be shed but I've learnt that there is a strength in vulnerability, a strength that only comes by being completely vulnerable to God. a strength that only God can provide.

It was a normal busy morning on the wards and just over 2 months into my hospital stay and a few days after my discharge from ICU. Mid-morning was the time when my body gave in to

It's Ok to Cry

the tiredness and I would lie with eyes closed listening to the bustle in the corridor and eventually doze.

The creak of the door opening disturbed that doze. The respiratory consultant walked in and sat by the bed. She was absolutely lovely, calm and serene, speaking softly and compassionately. As she talked though the floodgates opened and tears streamed down my face.

It was the first time that I had really cried since the Covid diagnosis. Yes, there had been a few tears when I was told that I was leaving ICU and going to the ward - but this felt different. The enormity of what I had just gone through began to hit home, but at the same time it felt surreal hearing what my body had gone through. 56 days in ICU and a "Do Not Resuscitate" order had been placed on my life - I was only 49! I knew that this decision would not have been taken lightly by the doctors and it only served as a reminder of the gravity of my condition.

Furiously wiping the tears away as they cascaded down my face, I gladly took the tissues offered by the doctor, apologising profusely for crying. Reassurance was her gift to me - this was a natural response, a process in the recovery. It was okay to cry.

She left the room leaving me to the thoughts that were whirling around my head. So, if this was a normal response then why did I feel so guilty for crying. Here I was, alive but crying, when so many others had lost their lives. Families grieving and wishing they could turn back the clock, wishing that they could see and hug their loved ones even one more time. Yet I had been given a second chance of life and my family would get that opportunity to see and hug me again.

Even though I knew this was the enemy's attempt at bringing me down with condemnation, it still tried to rear its ugly head.

'Jesus wept'.

Like lightening, the shortest verse in the Bible had been swung like a sword and shredded these thoughts to nothing. It felt like Jesus had leaned in and whispered in my ear, 'Its okay, its okay. Just cry'.

That's exactly what I did - again. The tears flowed but this time it wasn't because of guilt but of relief and gratitude that God had brought me through from the clutches of death itself.

In His love He wanted me to know that I didn't have to beat myself up over crying or thinking that I wasn't trusting Him to get me through this. In spite of my upbringing which had the motto 'You just get on with things' being deeply rooted in my thinking, God in His love and goodness was showing me that this was not the case. It was a lie. He didn't expect me to just get on with things. This was life changing and it would take time to process the enormity of what had happened. At that point my thinking was changed. Any part of my life where self-reliance remained was handed over to God lying in that bed. I was completely dependent on Him.

For the remainder of the day the Holy Spirit continued to comfort and bring passages of scripture to my mind. At this

It's Ok to Cry

point I had no Bible or mobile phone with me because I couldn't lift them or even try to turn over the pages. It was total reliance on the Holy Spirit who brought the scriptures to me, comforting, encouraging and teaching me.

One of the passages which proved invaluable is found in 1st Samuel chapter 30 where David and his men had returned to Ziglag only to find that their women and children had been taken captive by the enemy and the place burnt to the ground. They were faced with the charred remains of their life. The hope of coming home to family and resuming their life was in ashes.

These were strong men, burly men, warriors. They fought in battles but here they found themselves in the worst battle which they had ever faced. There was no rallying cry or speech. Instead these mighty warriors cried - really cried. I can just imagine the sound of them wailing, the raw emotion, even anger at their loss, reverberating around that village.

With the Bible describing that they cried until they had no more strength left to cry, how long would that be - a few hours, a day, a few days? Whatever the length of time, it conveys the depth of their despair. At this moment there was no holding back their emotions. In difficult seasons we should allow ourselves to cry rather than quickly wipe away tears and saying everything is fine.

I've discovered over the years and especially through this season that it is what we do in the moment which counts. There are always choices to make at these times - some good and others not - both of which can be seen here with David's men plotting to kill him. Alternatively, David, when he was faced with the choice of continuing to get caught up in the despair or to move forward and take the next step with God, he chose the latter.

I was also faced with this choice. How was I going to respond to what the Holy Spirit was revealing to me? In the natural it would have been so easy to lie and feel sorrow for myself but looking at what David and his men went through made me determined to go forward with God. After all it was Jesus who had stood by my bed watching over me while I was in the coma. It was God who kept me alive and brought me from the brink of death and He was the One who was going to walk with me through this.

I had a hope that this season will pass. Why? Because it's a basic principle which is described in Ecclesiastes that there is a time and a season for everything in life. I also really love that its specific, especially in chapter three and verse three, which says that there is a time to cry and a time to laugh. I was looking forward to that time of laughter which would herald in the new season, unnoticed at first but like the seasons which come and go every year its evident that change has happened.

From the full bloom of flowers in summer to the emptiness of winter, there is the knowledge that springtime will come with its new growth of buds and leaves bringing new hope of better days ahead. Better days were coming. It wasn't going to be easy, but the key was to navigate it with God just as David did.

The Bible says that he encouraged himself in the Lord and then went on to ask for a strategy and that's exactly what I did. This is the strategy which I have used based on this passage of scripture.

- Tell God how you feel.
- Remember what God has done for you in the past.
- Ponder Gods nature - His goodness, His Faithfulness, His Love.
- Ask God for help.
- Follow the direction He gives you.

What this looks like will be different for everybody, but God will give each person a step-by-step plan if you ask Him to.

Does it mean that I never cried after this? Certainly not! He knows when I cry and He will never turn His back on me or ignore me because I am upset. David knew this and wrote the words of Psalms 56:

'You keep track of all my sorrows,
You have collected all my tears in Your bottle
You have recorded each one of them in Your book'
(Psalm 56:8 NLT).

I made up my mind that no matter what would happen, I would choose joy and be grateful for every day that passed, even on the days when the tears flowed. I've always remembered Pastor Hilary in my church speaking on Habakkuk 3:17-19 where it describes a dire situation, but there was a decision made in verse 18 to rejoice in God. I love that reminder that no matter how difficult the circumstances that I can still rejoice because God is my strength.

Look at what happened to David once he moved on with God. God restored him and all that he had lost and God can still do that today. He never changes and He never will. That is why I am confident that God will bring about all that He has promised me. The season will change from winter, to spring and into the fullness and beauty of summer.

What God has done for me He will do for you. Trust God and His Word, ask Him for a plan, watch as He will restore your situations and you can move on from loss and weeping, to joy.

Remember in the process that ITS OK TO CRY.

Chapter 9

GOD GOALS

The tears quickly faded. I didn't have time to wallow in any self-pity. The reality of my condition no longer felt completely overwhelming. Inside me a spark had ignited - a fierce determination. One where I would approach each day with a warrior attitude, where I would tackle every hurdle head-on and I would try to remain joyful in the process.

Every day I checked in with my Commander, the One who had already promised the victory. It always gave me a giggle when I was talking out loud to the empty room and somebody walked in - but I didn't care. To me it was if He was sitting in the seat by the window. I know He heard and understood how difficult it was for me to be in bed 24/7 and having to re-learn the basics in living. He was still my constant companion even in a hospital room but I just wanted my home now. To be away from the hospital and its routine and to distance myself from the events of the past few months.

How was I going to get through this next stage of the journey and keep my sanity and determination intact?

That's when God set goals for me - each goal had its challenges to overcome, but I was relying on Him. The following goals did not look possible when I got them. I couldn't even scratch my nose let alone eat or lift a cup. There was no indication of how long I would need to be on the ward or in what condition I would be on discharge. My hope was centred on Him that I would achieve the following stages of recovery to get home:

- The ward
- The discharge
- The rehab
- Home for Christmas.

The ward - the first hurdle. Well, what can I say? If you have ever been unfortunate enough to be a patient and spend time in hospital you will know what it feels like.

The days are LONGGGGGGGGGGGG!

There is the rude early morning awakening around 5.30-6am followed by breakfast. By this stage over two hours had passed, I had been washed, changed and ready for another sleep when the breakfast trolley rattled up the corridor. The ability to eat had been affected with the length of time in the coma.

As I wasn't able to eat at first, the swallowing reflex had to be assessed at intervals by the speech and language therapist. All I was allowed were teaspoons of custard or pureed porridge before progressing to Weetabix and finally drinking water. However, it came with a stark warning that any coughing at any point while 'eating' had to be reported to the staff who would then contact the therapist. The risk of aspiration was a strong possibility which would mean a tube back into my stomach.

Gingerly I chewed that custard and pureed porridge with every teaspoon! I know custard really cannot be chewed but I did it with the miniscule amount on the spoon. Progress then came in the form of the pureed dinners. I cannot describe to you how I felt when my first pureed meal was set down in front of me. The menu had limited options of chicken curry, lasagne, fish pie or cottage pie. Have you ever seen these meals pureed, let alone eaten them? I'm sure my face gave away exactly what I was thinking when I looked at the first plastic container dinner which was set in front of me. I looked that container straight in the eye, took a deep breath and went for it.

Think bush tucker trial. That's what I did every time the food came until the day it was fish pie. Fish is supposed to be steamed or in batter, not swimming in a gloopy white sauce. No matter how much I eye-balled it I could not bring myself to taste it. Instead, I dreamt about getting a fish supper with all the condiments- salt, vinegar, tomato ketchup, bread and butter and a cup of tea to wash it all down. I could almost smell it, but that would have to wait until I could eat proper food again.

Every meal that I managed to eat was a meal closer to normal food. I missed the fruit I liked, the stir fries and roast chicken dinners, but when the speech and language therapist came holding a banana, I was ecstatic. Breaking a small piece off, she handed it to me and stood and watched. Ever so carefully I chewed this piece until it could not be chewed anymore. Slowly I swallowed. I was sure that it could be swallowed. Down it went.

There was no choking or coughing afterwards. We waited, as sometimes the coughing took a little while before occurring. It felt like forever. Finally, she was convinced that this had been successfully swallowed and I was put onto the next stage. To top it all she left the banana for me to finish!!! I was SO excited!

I munched that banana, savouring every bite of it. I was getting so near but yet so far at eating normally. It was difficult trying to remain patient and to stick with it and not jump ahead of what the plan was. Thankfully, the patience paid off until the ultimate prize came - well in terms of hospital food anyway – TOAST. And not just toast, but buttered toast.

It was teatime and the smell of toast was wafting down the corridor when the therapist brought in a plate with that coveted slice. As she sat it down in front of me, I had to resist the urge to shove a large piece into my mouth.

I carefully bit a piece off.

I began to chew.

It tasted amazing.

I chewed and chewed and chewed.

I ATE THE REST OF THAT TOAST!

I HAD PASSED THE TEST!

I was able to give up the pureed meals and go onto the ever-anticipated toast and normal diet. It didn't matter that I couldn't hold a knife and fork for a spoon was all I could manage, but I was ecstatic.

The next challenge was to be able to move. I had the expertise of the physiotherapist and grit and determination within me. While I had been in ICU, the physiotherapists had worked to get me to sit upright at the side of bed. At the start I couldn't even support my head. It just flopped forward like a rag doll.

I was horrified. I would become so breathless that everything around me started to go black. It was brutal. They even tried to get me to stand for a few seconds but all seemed impossible. My legs were like jelly, my head floppy, I was breathless and then I would get nauseated and vomit. There are just no words to describe how brutal it was. I hated it. It felt like torture. The usual line from the therapists were that if I wanted to go home to my family then I had to do it.

One day I had just had enough of being reminded that I was away from my family. I was so frustrated at being in this position. How could they even think that I wanted to be in that unit a second longer than I needed to be? The moment they walked around the curtain and started talking of moving and getting home, that was my opening to say a few points politely.

Thankfully the nurse had heard them the previous few occasions and hovered around the bed while I explained how their words were not motivating, but that it was playing on patients' emotions in a negative way. I was 49 - I wanted to go home to my family. I didn't want to be in a unit that was like sitting in a waiting room to Death Valley.

They left, leaving me alone to reflect on where I was going, what needed to be accomplished and alone to talk it over with God. There are so many Bible verses which were Gods promises to me for walking again, which continued to encourage and strengthen me.

Now back on the ward, the process of gaining mobility continued. My neck was stronger and it no longer flopped forward when I sat forward from the pillow. Eventually I was able to sit at the side of the bed attached to oxygen and with three people holding me.

Slowly this progressed to standing up for a few seconds before they gently set me back down on the bed. I always felt that progress was too slow during this time, but in hindsight the opposite was true. God was surpassing all the medical teams' expectations. I was able to progress to use a contraption called the 'steady' (which had a small platform on wheels and bars attached at front to hold. It still took two or three people but my job was to grab hold of the bars and try and pull myself up. It was going to take a while but every second which I stood was an achievement.

The staff aimed at being able to wheel me over to the nearby chair at the window so that I could sit out for periods during the day. Everyday a bigger goal was set by increasing the time sitting out as the talk of carers became more frequent. The nurses explained that four hours was the target because of the time between carers' visits. I can say I wasn't a fan of having carers, but at this point it was a sensible option to discuss.

Once again God did the impossible and I was sitting out most days between four and seven hours. It was exhausting and painful, but I did it. It was another victory over the enemy and another step closer to home.

I was far from being able to walk but at least I could be transferred from a bed to a chair.

The next hurdle was being able to progress with personal care. For that I needed help. There was no escaping, but as I regained some movement in my fingers, I was able to wash my face when handed a facecloth. This was a huge achievement. With all of this going on, I spent the afternoons trying to recover from the morning activities. I would usually sleep before watching some television but I quickly tired of this.

I then had a brilliant idea! Much to the amusement of my two visitors, I became focused on making a Christmas present list. After all it was now into October and normally by this time of year I would have all the presents bought and often wrapped. Visiting time became like a committee meeting on what to buy and for whom, with my sister and daughter being dispatched to bring home the goods. All I had to do was give them the details and mentally tick it off the list in my head. It would have been so nice to have the usual dedicated notebook and pen, but that would wait until I could write again.

It seemed that every few days there was an update from my shoppers with pictures taken of what they had bought.

Then it moved onto Christmas dinner!! This entailed what would we have, what would be left out and where would I be? Would there be any way of getting out to a house?

SUDDENLY

Suddenly I was being told that I had been declared medically fit for discharge home. I was in disbelief.

There were two choices available – I could go into a nursing home or home with a care package. Thankfully my sister was a great advocate and pointed out that a nursing home was not an option – that it would be detrimental to my recovery and mental well-being. Gwyneth, my sister, and Judith, my daughter and I had many discussions of how it would all work. All the equipment had been ordered – the hospital bed, oxygen tanks, a 'steady', hospital chair, table and commode.

Unfortunately, the reality soon hit that it could take six weeks or more for a care package to be available. Yet my bed was needed now. I couldn't wait six weeks.

The decision was made that I was going to go home to my sister, to family. Once we had told this decision to the staff, an ambulance was booked for within a matter of days. It was a flurry of activity with me sending home my belongings and leaving only the essentials.

The day of departure arrived. The ambulance was booked for five o'clock. The hours dragged, but it didn't dampen my excitement at all.

Suddenly, two hours earlier than expected, the two ambulance personnel arrived at my room.

"Was I ready?" they asked.

I eagerly nodded. After all I had been ready for this moment since I was first admitted! I was lifted into the wheelchair and as quietly as I arrived on the ward, on a night three months prior, I quietly left.

I didn't look behind as I was wheeled along the corridors towards the exit. What was ahead of me would be better than the past few months. And with that I went through the doors and into the outside world.

Hope in the Valley

Chapter 10

PIGS AND WINDMILLS

I breathed in. The fresh air entered my airways. In that second of being outside, my heart was full - full of joy, relief, hope and gratitude.

I was alive!

Finally, I had made it out of the building which had been my residence for the past three months.

The autumn sun was shining and there was a crispness to the air but it wasn't cold. If it was, I didn't feel it as I was being pushed onto the ambulance. My stomach had butterflies in it - a mixture of excitement and apprehension about the next stage of this journey. The confines of the hospital were about to be swapped for the comfort of my sister's home. Everything that had become familiar over the past months were now gone along with the security of a nursing/medical team present 24/7.

I was entering unfamiliar territory.

The wheelchair came to a standstill in the back of the ambulance, the chains clunked and clicked as the paramedic secured the wheelchair into place.

Slowly, ever so slowly, the ambulance made its way to the exit before stopping at the red traffic lights.

It was late Friday afternoon and the traffic congestion had already begun. This journey was going to take a bit longer than I had anticipated. It wasn't exactly the pig and windmill moment which I had dreamt of but that was okay.

If you are wondering about the connection of pig and windmills let me, tell you. When I was back on the ward and able to send messages to my family, the main talk centred around coming home. I came across an image which had a pig with an excited grin on its face while hanging out of the back car window holding a windmill. There was a caption saying, 'I'M COMING HOME'.

It just seemed to capture what I felt about going home. Once I had shared it with my family, it became the standard picture which we used when anything about my discharge was mentioned. There was a bit of a flaw though in the image - I wasn't in the back of a car with family collecting me and I wasn't able to walk.

Even if it didn't play out as I had imagined, it didn't matter now as I was being pushed up the driveway and lifted up the steps into the house. There to meet me was my husband Mark, my sister Gwyneth and daughters, Judith and Sophie. The look of relief and happiness on their faces was priceless - a stark contrast to the previous ambulance journey.

This was the moment that we had prayed and believed God for.

The living room was ready for me - the dark brown hospital chair stuck out like a sore thumb from the rest of the décor. It was high backed, with a bare steel frame coated in dark brown paint. It wasn't comfortable but it was a necessity so that I could be lifted up out of it easily. The oxygen cylinder was placed beside it ready to be switched on after the exertion of moving.

It all felt a bit surreal, overwhelming in fact.

Thankfully there wasn't much time to dwell on that as the rest of the family arrived, bringing WINDMILLS!!

There was a windmill for everyone.

The room erupted into cheering and clapping, lots of hugs being given and lots of chatter. It was a noisy affair which would mark a new chapter in my recovery.

Whether everyone had been well warned by Gwyneth to keep the length of visit to a minimum or the 'nod' was given to indicate it was time to leave, I still don't know. Almost simultaneously each one got up, said their goodbyes and left.

The front door was shut and quietness descended upon the living room.

The excitement and adrenaline of the past few hours were catching up on me and tiredness was creeping in. There was a drawback to having a nurse as a sister - I couldn't hide the fatigue from her. Off she went and returned with the 'steady' and despite my protests, I was going to bed. It had been a long day, but worth it.

I was in my niece's bedroom, next door to my sister. The hospital bed was waiting for my arrival. I kept looking around the room and grinning to myself. Then at some point I remembered my niece, Chloe, giving vent to her feelings about the spiders in her room. I remember looking at the wall beside my bed to check for spiders and thinking if a spider appeared I wouldn't be able to do anything about it because I couldn't move much in the bed and my hands hadn't recovered movement yet.

Being a bit dramatic, I then decided that the spider would be able to come off the wall and land on top of me. Obviously it would do a bungee jump to achieve this, so I spent the next hour on spider watch. At some point tiredness took over and the spider watch abruptly ended.

Upon waking up the next morning, I was extremely pleased to find that no spiders had bungee jumped onto the bed. At least it gave my sister much amusement when I told her about it during breakfast. That set the tone for the rest of my stay with her – that of laughter and lots of it – if there was something to laugh at, we found it. After all it does say in the Bible that a merry heart is good medicine!

With no carers' package available, the onus lay on my family to provide round-the-clock care. At least there were no 5am wake up calls for blood pressures or getting washed. It was all now very civilised – a cup of tea was had before the wash. My sister would come in grinning with the basin filled with hot water and a facecloth. The face cloth was covered with the dove shower gel which was then walloped around me causing a mass of soap suds. Then I was wheeled into the living room ready to face the day ahead.

I was happy with that UNTIL the topic of conversation became focused on washing my hair. The only way it could be done was lying in bed. My daughter Judith had the perfect solution. I will refer to it as the 'paddling pool for the head'. It was a white square blow-up with a dip on one edge that allowed it to be placed under the neck. Easy enough you would think. Well, in one respect it was easier than the hard basin which was used under my head in hospital. However, the first attempt of doing my hair was absolutely hilarious.

Gwyneth ran with the jugs of water from bathroom to bedroom, while Judith was tasked with the actual washing of my hair. The water poured over my hair, face, neck - anywhere really, with me spluttering and laughing and her squealing. This is exactly how a hair wash day went. It was even funnier at subsequent hair washes when Judith exclaimed – "I'll not soak

Hope in the Valley

you today" – and usually within seconds of that first water jug being poured I was in fact soaked and spluttering while she squealed with laughter.

Meanwhile, as all evidence of being drenched was being cleared away, Gwyneth was unleashed with the hairdryer and at one point also the hair curlers. Much to her delight, I wasn't able to get up and run away. This was a very stark contrast to my own hair routine which I had followed at home which involved a quick wash hair, towel dry and go, with only the occasional use of the hairdryer. No spending ages blow-drying, let alone straighteners or tongs. Any protests of mine fell on deaf ears! I realised early on that it was quicker to be quiet - it also meant that the kettle would be boiled earlier for that necessary mid-morning cuppa.

So, the learning curve continued.

"The steady" was the contraption needed to transport me around the house. There is no easy way to explain it so I won't even try. What I will say is at least it was in my favourite colour which is purple. None of my family had used this before, so with a quick lesson my sister was braced and ready to go. Judith was given a quick demonstration from my sister.

"L" plates would have been useful as the turns were quite tight in the hallway and with a few dents in the skirting boards, this skill was mastered. Well, when I say mastered – there was still the odd calamity. On one occasion Gwyneth had wheeled me down to bed and bent down to take my shoes off.

Unfortunately, on the way back up she banged her head on the bars of the steady. If she saw stars, she didn't say but she did comment that maybe it would knock some sense into her. Before I had even realised, I quipped back, "It is too late for that," at which point we burst out laughing until the tears were rolling down our faces, me coughing, wheezing and laughing and having to sit even longer with the oxygen on.

Then there was the time when she was determined to bring me into the kitchen for a change of scene. The layout of the narrow hallway prevented a head-on approach over the brass room divider. Not to be defeated, Gwyneth came down the hallway picking up pace as we approached the kitchen. With one fast, strong push the steady was jolted over the divider and I had made it into the kitchen.

It was worth it though for the memories.

It wasn't all fun and laughter, but it was better to dwell on those memories than to get into a negative state of mind. After all, this stage in the recovery was about getting back home, walking and as independent as I was pre-covid.

There was nerve damage as a result of the duration of the coma. It meant that my feet felt like two bricks at the end of my legs. I had no feeling in my feet but when I felt them with my hands, they were stone cold. The side and front of both thighs, shins and calves were affected too, although they weren't totally numb. Multiple times throughout the day I would be poking at my legs to see if the feeling was returning.

Now that I was home there was nobody asking me to wiggle my toes, but I continued to wiggle them as many times as I could during the day. I was willing them to move, especially the big toe on my right foot. It was just floppy. I would flick it or try and hold it up, but nothing happened. It just flopped.

According to the experts, this polyneuropathy would affect the ability to walk. How much? Nobody knew.

There were moments when I had to really dig deep and not worry about the outcome. After all, God pulled me from the brink of death, so why would He not restore my mobility? God ensured that I had an experienced physiotherapist who was thorough, put me at ease and was encouraging. It would be lovely to say that it was all easy and straightforward, but it wasn't. The fatigue was real and some days it was a real battle to begin the exercises. On those days I had to have a stern conversation with myself. This was usually along the lines of, 'By failing to do them you would delay progress to be walking again and how would you feel about that?'

With family, thankfully there was no chance of forgetting to do the physiotherapy. On the days when my daughter Judith came over to give Gwyneth time to get out of the house, the car was barely out of the driveway when the question came, "Mum are you going to do your physio?"

There was no escape!

Judith was not one for listening to excuses!

The physiotherapy was completed and a full report given to my sister on return, with Judith always looking so pleased with herself.

I was well aware that recovery wasn't going to happen overnight. I had a responsibility and a part to play - rest, physio, eating well and not letting discouragement take a foothold. Every day I have a foot brace to wear to help strengthen the right foot which in turn will help with taking steps. Each day is a day to rely on God, to listen to His Word and stay encouraged in Him.

There were two particular Bible verses which I kept before me and continually spoke over my life, and I will continue to do so until I am walking again.

> *"For by You I can run against a troop, by my God I can leap over a wall"* (Psalm 18:29 NKJV)

On a daily basis, while sitting in the chair in my sister's living room, I would look out at the front garden at the waist high red brick wall. I would sit and imagine myself jumping over that wall into the street. Until that time comes, I will keep this verse and this image before me as a reminder of what will be.

The other verse says this:

> *"But those who wait on the Lord shall renew their strength, they shall mount up with wings like eagles, they shall run and not be weary, they shall walk and not faint"* (Isaiah 40:31 NKJV).

Hope in the Valley

    To this day those verses are my hope that when I walk again, I will walk with strength, unaided, and I will not be held back by distance or terrain. For my God keeps His promises so I keep trusting and looking forward to that day, grateful for the progress which I have made no matter how small and insignificant it may be.

Chapter 11

HOPE IN HIS GOODNESS

I was exhausted. Every part of my body ached. My head was sore. The shooting pains in my legs and feet was like a thousand knives stabbing me all at once. I winced with the pain. I just wanted to go to sleep. Even the normally soft pillows felt like bricks beneath my head. Yet the multiple pillows were necessary to keep me upright and help my breathing.

Gone was the usual duvet. Its weight now felt unbearable after the coma. In its place was a soft, lightweight fleece blanket which cocooned me.

The noise from the television drifted in from the living room, along with the chatter of my husband Mark and daughter Sophie. Beside me the dog was snoring, having wriggled his way under the blanket.

I lay looking around the dimly-lit room smiling to myself, for despite the exhaustion and pain I was happy, content and thankful.

What a day it had been. I closed my eyes and let the memories of Christmas swirl around in my mind.

Christmas – people either love it or hate it.

The debate over whether it is too early for shops to stock Christmas decorations, to put up Christmas trees and play seasonal music still persists. I remembered the years when I worked in a surgery and receptionists loved Christmas. Every August one of them would start a Christmas countdown in the big diary at reception. The Christmas tree was decorated in the waiting room and the 'secret' Santa draw took. When I say secret – we weren't secret about it - that part of the phrase was not stuck to at all. The presents were exchanged before anyone went off on holiday until finally the lights were turned off and the place deserted for the few days of bank holidays.

December holidays were always my favourite. It wasn't just about the presents, but the childhood memories of being at my aunt's home for Christmas dinner. I remembered the late-night shopping on a Thursday which was a treat, the helping to prepare soup, trifle and vegetables for the banquet. Then the handing out of presents before heading home.

The years may have passed but the excitement of spending the time with family has not waned. This year I was determined to have Christmas. For me it would look different from past years, but that was okay. I was so grateful that God had brought me this far.

No words can describe the feeling of waking up on Christmas day with your family and spending precious time with them at the holiday season. It was that image which spurred me on every day. I wanted to be in my own home with my two daughters and watch them open their presents.

I wanted to sit with the fire crackling and the Christmas tree lights twinkling in the darkness while the aroma of cinnamon from the candles wafted through the air. Gone was the smell of the homemade shortbread which was now boxed and ready to consume with copious amounts of tea. All of these things were the pre-cursor for the star attraction - the Christmas dinner.

Uncertainty loomed over whether this would be achievable. Some days it seemed more doable than others as I still required a high level of care.

I had pictured myself walking down my sisters' front steps and once we had pulled up in my driveway I would walk unaided up the steps into my own house. Reluctantly, I had to admit that this would not be achievable. Nonetheless there was a cause to celebrate because I was going home! The day I moved back home was a mixture of sadness at leaving my sister's house but also happiness that I would wake up with my children at Christmas.

It was all a bit surreal, even a bit frightening. For almost five months I had medical staff around me - first at hospital and then with my sister. If I even so much as shuffled about the bed at an unusual hour my sister, Gwyneth, was in at the bedside like a whippet. If my oxygen levels had dropped, she knew just by looking at me and plonked the oxygen on despite my protests.

Now I was home and the only person with nursing experience was myself. I remember sitting thinking, 'Now what?' when I first got home and was positioned on the recliner chair. It just wasn't what I had imagined but I couldn't pinpoint why.

That first evening of being home my husband Mark, who is a man of few words, just kept smiling over at me and saying, 'You are home'. I grinned back because even though he didn't say it I knew that he was glad to have me back. As a family we were entering uncharted territory. There was so much to think about - oxygen, physical help, keeping an eye on me during meal times as there was still the potential to choke and the night-time hours when I needed assistance. It took a few weeks to get into a routine, but thankfully we had the support of family who were in and out on a daily basis helping with housework, getting me washed and dressed, cooking meals and just coming in for a chat.

I found being home particularly frustrating because it felt like I was a stranger in my own home. It all just felt unfamiliar. While in hospital, Judith had sent me a picture of home and I looked at it bewildered. I didn't even remember what my street looked like, nor could I have described the house. I wracked my brain trying to remember what home looked like but it was futile until the day I actually came home. In my absence the bedroom had been beautifully re-decorated for my coming home – cosy, warm, inviting. It became my safe haven.

I turned my attention to getting ready for Christmas – or maybe I should re-phrase that - making sure everybody else in the house was getting ready.

First the Christmas tree, which was left for the girls to put up. They could have put it upside down and I would have been delighted. This year was not a year for me to be meticulously arranging the baubles in a colour co-ordinated manner, (much to their delight). They even suggested just covering the front of the tree, leaving the back empty, to which I readily agreed!!

Presents were next on the list – all of which had been sorted out by Gwyneth and Judith with Naomi being chief wrapper. One final check and everything was ready. With the smell of coffee, eating homemade shortbread and Christmas movies on in the background, Christmas Eve was here.

There was no smell of ham being cooked, stuffing being made or vegetables being prepared this year but that would wait for another time. I don't know how but before I knew it, I was being wheeled down to bed. Usually, I would wait until the girls went into bed and then distribute their presents in their selected seats. Instead, the instructions were given to Mark to do this. Now that the girls were older, they were up long after I went to bed but finally they closed their bedroom doors and quietness descended on the house.

It was after midnight now and I just could not get to sleep.

PING

PING

I reached out for my phone and looked at the messages expecting a 'Happy Christmas' to be there (as is the norm in our family if anyone is awake just after midnight on Christmas Eve).

It was my eldest daughter Judith. She had formed a family group on her phone at 1:15am titled 'Christmas' with her, Sophie and I as the members. The conversation went as follows:

Judith: "Who's awake?" (1.15am)

Me: "Me"

Judith: "Sophie?" (1:16am)

Me: "Everyone sleeping except us" (1:17am)

Sophie: "Oh me, Hi, am I late?" (1:34am)

Judith: "No, Hello"

Me: Sends a waving hand

Judith: Sends a present emoji (1.35am)

Judith: "Are we opening?" (1.36am)

The rest is history. With much stifled giggling, the girls emerged from their rooms to find me, got me up and into the living room. The Christmas tree lights were switched on, the heating was put on, I was put in my chair and we were ready.

The 'Santa' presents were given out, we talked, laughed, drank tea and hot chocolate. The dogs trotted about sniffing the presents and waiting to see if they would get any snacks. A few hours later, off went the Christmas tree lights and the heating and I was taken back to bed. I lay for the first while chuckling to myself at the antics and the randomness of it all especially because Mark was lying snoring oblivious to all that had gone on.

This may not have seemed a big thing to many but for me it was everything. Why? Because I didn't miss the girls opening their presents. It was another prayer answered by a loving God who gave me in that moment the desire of my heart in a most random way - that even months later it still makes me smile at the preciousness of that moment.

This time we all settled and before long I was sleeping content in the knowledge that the rest of the day was going to exceed all expectations all because of a God who loves me.

Once awake again the family got me washed, dressed and hair done. I was exhausted. As I looked around me at all the faces though, my heart was just bursting with happiness. The kitchen windows were steamed up with all the food cooking despite the windows being open, the table was set and here I was – sitting with my family.

I had made it.

Christmas dinner is always a noisy affair with us. The clattering of plates and pots as the food is served, the bang of crackers being pulled and the cheesy jokes being told. Everyone talking over each other and trying to keep up with everyone's conversations. The food cooked by my sister as always was delicious - and I was able to manage it!

This year two six-month-old golden retrievers were in tow joining in the celebrations, happy at all the attention which they were receiving and delighted of course with their bowl of turkey dinner. With tails wagging, they joined the rush to get a comfy chair in the living room. No rush for me though as my chair was reserved! Not wanting to be left out the dogs clambered up on a few knees - the stars of the show.

If the dinner was meant to make them sleepy it failed miserably, because now it was present time. Gwyneth took on the role as the master of ceremonies and the presents were handed out as we all applauded and watched everyone opening the presents with the OOOOs and AHHHs filling the room and of course lots of hugs.

Meanwhile, the dogs obviously decided that us humans were having way too much fun. As the rest of the afternoon progressed, the house was filled with chatting, squeals of laughter and dogs bounding about and ripping the wrapping paper which had been discarded on the floor. It may have looked like chaos at times, but the most important ingredient of the day filled the room - love. The love of family - a family united at Christmas. A family so thankful because only three months prior all hope was disappearing and an empty seat at the table was becoming ever more likely.

God however was in the equation and it was only by His grace and His strength that I was sitting there. It was a testimony to those around the table but most of all me that God is the God of hope. There have been tears and laughter along the way, but that was a day of laughter and joy. It was a day for celebrating the birth of a Saviour, a day which reminded us that the God who promised it in His Word had done what He said He would do. The God who is able to do exceedingly, abundantly above all that we can think ask or dare to dream (Ephesians 3:20 New King James).

The day was over for me by 6pm and it was home to bed, exhausted but happy. Tomorrow, Boxing Day, would be spent at home this year which suited us perfectly. I slept for fifteen hours solid. My day was filled with gratitude of what God had done for me. He gave me not only my life back but filled it with His goodness.

I am just so thankful for this memory and wanted to share a snapshot of that time because I feel that it's a reflection of what God does. He didn't just bring me to a stage of getting home and forgetting about me but He saw to it that in amongst the difficult days there would be memories which would bring joy, laughter and hope - memories which would last a lifetime. His goodness flooded my life.

Was now too early to think about next Christmas? Maybe, but I know that it will exceed all expectation just as this Christmas had.

Hope in the Valley

Chapter 12

DARE TO HOPE

Could there be a normal life after Covid? If so, what would it look like for me?

That question raced through my mind. Every day was a day closer to recovery, but my progress had dwindled, leaving me to reflect on what would be. I wanted to be able to live life without the many complications which Covid had brought - the exhaustion, the pain of nerve damage, insomnia, lack of independence and cysts on my lungs. I could continue to list all the negatives but one day I read the verse below and it struck me to the core:

> *"I will never forget this awful time as I grieve over my loss,*
> YET I STILL DARE TO HOPE *when I remember this:*

The faithful love of the Lord never ends".
Lamentations chapter 3:20-22 (New Living Translation)

This verse encapsulated how I felt over the past fourteen months of my life. It will certainly be a time which will be remembered by myself and my family and friends as an awful time. For me this time will be like a memorial which has been erected on the timeline of my life: a defining moment which would carve out the beginning of a new chapter in my life.

Despite the memory, despite being able to grieve over all that had been lost, I could remain hopeful.

Yes, I had to be responsible and ensure that I continued to do whatever was necessary for recovery. I had to eat well, regain lost muscle and continue with the physio exercises. The progress may be slow but if I stayed consistent, I knew that I would reap the rewards over time.

As I mulled this verse over, I love that the reason for hope is made clear. It is because of the everlasting, faithful love of God. This is why I can hope for the future regardless of what it looks like now, because God Himself is love and it is the essence of Who He is.

It is a love which has been expressed since the beginning of time, the creation of man and it is the same love which is available today through Jesus Christ who willingly gave His life as the ransom for our sin. Only the love of a Father so deep and the love of a Son so great could break that sin barrier and provide a way for us to be back into relationship with God. The words in the book of Romans chapter eight describes that not even death itself has the power to separate us from the love of God.

I have walked through that valley of the shadow of death and experienced His love and His presence every step of the journey. No matter what life looks like I am surrounded by the love of God and that alone is a reason to wake up every day and smile, secure in the knowledge that that I am loved by Almighty God.

It is that love from a God who never changes, who is the only constant in my life and who is the foundation for every promise in the Bible. When I read verses in the Bible such as Psalm 71:5 which says,

"For you are my hope O Lord God," then I know that this promise of hope comes from God alone. It transcends human reasoning and it results in hopeless situations being transformed.

Throughout the Bible there are so many accounts of where hope comes in place of trouble. One of my favourites is the story of Hannah which is found in 1st Samuel chapter 5. Hannah had no children and this was considered a curse in the ancient world. As a result, Hannah became the object of scorn and ridicule for years. Upset, distraught and probably losing hope she did what she knew to do. She called out to God during the yearly visit to the temple and asked God specifically for a son.

There is no doubt in my mind of her distress and anguish because as she pours her heart out to God, Eli the priest in the temple thought that she was drunk. I just love the response of Hannah when Eli tells her that God had granted her petition. She was able to eat again because she was not sad anymore!

This woman had come in despondent, ridiculed, bullied and broken by the years of abuse yet she looked to God. She went in despondent and came out delighted. Her heart was now joyful and peaceful as she went her way and waited for Gods promise to be reality in her life.

> *"Now may the God of HOPE fill you with all joy and peace in believing, that you may abound in hope by the power of the Holy Spirit".* (Romans 15:8, NIV)

God stepped into Hannah's pain and not only did she have son called Samuel but she went on to have three sons and two daughters (1Samuel 2:21). God restored Hannah's life and gave her immeasurably more than she could have ever imagined. Her story encapsulates all that God is – love, faithfulness and the restorer of lives.

Taking encouragement from Hannah's story meant that regardless of the daily struggles and frustrations which I had to endure, I could completely rest on His love and His promises that life would improve. Yet it is in the journey and battles of life that I believe that you can discover things about yourself, your relationship with God and what you are building your life on.

For me it has been a process which has involved participating with the Holy Spirit and allowing Him to guide, teach and minister to me during this time. It has required me being completely vulnerable in all aspects of life and open to His correction and guidance. One of the biggest lessons for me was to completely depend on God for and with everything. Not just the 'big things' in life but even the most miniscule detail. I was dependent for the very life in my body but I was also dependent on the tiniest details such as having someone to scratch my nose.

Was I not depending on God prior to Covid? The answer to that would be a "Yes" but what I learnt in those raw honest times with Holy Spirit was that I still had a measure of self-reliance. What I have experienced is that when all is literally stripped away - what or rather Who will you depend on?

Will you depend on yourself, your job, your income, or a high position within your chosen career or influence within your town? Can I just say that if you are, that NONE of that matters when your life is hanging in the balance? The only thing that matters is having a personal relationship with the Lord Jesus and giving Him full access to all areas in your life.

Everything I had or was had been completely stripped away while I was in hospital - independence, dignity, career and ability to function at an optimal level in order to live a full life. In the days of trying to cope with loss and to an extent grieving over what had been lost I cried and I struggled, but through it all the Lord was faithful.

It wasn't because of myself. It was all God and the moment that I took my focus off myself and how awful the situation was onto a focus of being grateful for all that God was doing and all that He would continue to do, then that sense of loss diminished. In its place was a fresh hope for the future, a fresh desire to dream again, a burning desire to serve God and see lives transformed in His presence.

Now every day is a fresh opportunity to be thankful to God for the small things in life. To lie in bed at night with the blinds open and look at the moon shining into the bedroom. To wake up and have breath is something I will remain thankful for. To wake up and hear the sparrows chirping out in the garden is a moment to be thankful.

To wake up in the morning and find the dog lying on top of my head or him pulling the duvet off me so he could get underneath it is a moment to be thankful. To wake up and be able to speak to family and be able to hug them is a moment to be thankful.

It says that in everything we should give thanks to God – even when life is not going to plan. Even on the days when the fatigue is crippling, when the flashbacks occur and sleep is nowhere to be seen I will still be thankful. I will be thankful that I have my bed to sleep in, that I can depend on God to bring sleep and rest to my body and for His peace over my mind.

I believe that this will change in time because of the promise which is found in Jeremiah 30:17 where it reads that God '*will restore health to you and heal you of your wounds' (NKJV).* I am looking forward to see that promise of restoration come to pass in my life. God is a God of restoration and those promises are what fills me with hope that the future will look different to the season that I am coming out of.

For me the journey and process continue. I feel that it is so important to remember that this is not what defines me as a person. I am not a victim in this. I am an overcomer through Jesus Christ, a conqueror who has gone through the battle and emerged victorious. When we walk in victory our challenges don't instantly disappear, but it means that we have decided to not allow them to consume us.

Whatever my life looks like I know that the Lord is always faithful. I have a better future because of the One in whom I have placed my hope - a hope that is steadfast, a hope that is fully persuaded in the source of Hope - God Himself.

And so, to the future….

So far, my journey has seen me away from work due to the illness, in the clutches of death, and experiencing the miraculous power of God who has sustained my life and throughout the recovery process.

I am still in the recovery process and I firmly believe that there will be complete recovery. I believe that there will be a full restoration of my health and all that I have lost during this season of my life. I believe that there will be a recompense - that what the enemy has taken will be given back to me again.

In Isaiah 43:18,19 it says this:

"Do not remember the former things, nor consider the things of old, Behold I am doing a new thing".

This verse is a reminder that I go forward and turn my attention on what is ahead, not on what has been. If I were to continue in looking behind me, then I will miss what God is doing now in my life.

So where do I go from here?

Living a life unhindered is the goal.

For me, firstly that means being able to walk again and be independent and not be reliant on other people to help me around.

The next would be a life full of vitality and for exhaustion to be a thing of the past. In the meantime, I know that each hour that I sleep, my body is recovering. I have moved on from the frustration and even anger at being so tired. I have to be sensible about my limitations at present, but again I know that this too shall pass.

A life without the oxygen bottle - no 'jet pack' to be put on my back to go out in the car with family – or oxygen bottles in various rooms in the house. Even lighting the fire will be easier without family running to remove the oxygen bottles from the room!

For me my future is indeed looking great. How could it not with God by my side?

This book is only the beginning.

It is a time to revisit the dreams that have been buried over the years due to life circumstances. What is it that I have dreamt of, how can I achieve it? Are there some things which I need to let go of? Only God knows and I trust Him for His direction and guidance.

I'm excited for all that God will do in my life. I really feel that this has been a defining moment for me. No longer will I be held back by fear of the unknown or fear of failure. Instead, I intend to march forward with my head held high. I will go in the direction He leads and fulfil the plan that God has for me. Opportunities are there all around and it's time to grab them and run with them as God directs.

Fresh fire, fresh vision. Fresh anointing.

A life lived to the full for Jesus.

A hope that there will be better days ahead because I am connected to the source of hope - God.

Maybe you find yourself in a valley situation and don't know what to do or how it will improve. I trust that this book will bring encouragement to you that there is always hope. There are no limits with God.

Hope in the Valley

Lift up your eyes and gaze on the One who will never fail you, the One who is faithful, the One who loves you unconditionally.

You too will find that there is *Hope in the Valley*.

Printed in Great Britain
by Amazon